First World War
and Army of Occupation
War Diary
France, Belgium and Germany

57 DIVISION
170 Infantry Brigade,
Brigade Machine Gun Company
9 February 1917 - 28 February 1918

WO95/2979/9

The Naval & Military Press Ltd
www.nmarchive.com
Published in association with The National Archives

Published by

The Naval & Military Press Ltd

Unit 10 Ridgewood Industrial Park,

Uckfield, East Sussex,

TN22 5QE England

Tel: +44 (0) 1825 749494

www.naval-military-press.com

www.nmarchive.com

This diary has been reprinted in facsimile from the original. Any imperfections are inevitably reproduced and the quality may fall short of modern type and cartographic standards.

© **Crown Copyright**
Images reproduced by permission of The National Archives, London, England, 2015.

Contents

Document type	Place/Title	Date From	Date To
Heading	WO95/2979-9		
Heading	57th Division 170th Infy Bde 170th Machine Gun Coy Feb 1917-Feb 1918		
Miscellaneous	O.C. 170 Machine Gun Company	04/05/1917	04/05/1917
War Diary		09/02/1917	18/02/1917
War Diary	Cordonnerie Sector	18/02/1917	28/02/1917
Miscellaneous	O.C. 170 Machine Gun Company	31/03/1917	31/03/1917
War Diary	Cordonnerie Sector	01/03/1917	01/03/1917
War Diary	Sailly	02/03/1917	03/03/1917
War Diary	Cordonnerie Sector	04/03/1917	31/03/1917
Miscellaneous	Machine Gun Company	01/05/1917	01/05/1917
War Diary	Cordonnerie Sector	01/04/1917	23/04/1917
War Diary	Cordonnerie-Boutillerie Sector	24/04/1917	31/05/1917
Miscellaneous	Machine Gun Company	01/07/1917	01/07/1917
War Diary	Cordonnerie-Boutillerie Sector	01/06/1917	05/08/1917
War Diary	Armentieres Sector	05/08/1917	31/08/1917
Miscellaneous	Headquarters 57th Division	03/10/1917	03/10/1917
War Diary	Armentieres	01/09/1917	15/09/1917
War Diary	Armentieres Jesus Farm Camp B.20.a.20.80	16/09/1917	18/09/1917
War Diary	Form B, 20a. 20.80 La Gorgue	18/09/1917	18/09/1917
War Diary	L.28.c.2070. To Busnes At P.31.c.60.40	19/09/1917	19/09/1917
War Diary	To La Tirmande S.6.a.25.30	20/09/1917	26/09/1917
War Diary	La-Tiremande	27/09/1917	17/10/1917
War Diary	Renescure	18/10/1917	18/10/1917
War Diary	Proven	19/10/1917	23/10/1917
War Diary	Pilkem-Ridge	24/10/1917	27/10/1917
War Diary	Proven	28/10/1917	31/10/1917
Miscellaneous	Headquarters 57th Division	01/12/1917	01/12/1917
War Diary	Proven	01/11/1917	07/11/1917
War Diary	Licques	08/11/1917	14/11/1917
War Diary	Ecottes	15/11/1917	30/11/1917
Miscellaneous	Herewith War Diary For Month Of December 1917	03/01/1918	03/01/1918
War Diary	Ecottes	01/12/1917	08/12/1917
War Diary	Proven	09/12/1917	12/12/1917
War Diary	Rousbrugge	13/12/1917	15/12/1917
War Diary	Boesinghe Area	16/12/1917	31/12/1917
War Diary	Proven Area	01/01/1918	02/01/1918
War Diary	Erquinghem	03/01/1918	03/01/1918
War Diary	Wez Macquart Sector	04/01/1918	28/02/1918
War Diary	Estaires		
Miscellaneous	B.E.F. France & Flanders		

2015/2979 (c) mom

2017/2979 (c) mom

57TH DIVISION
170TH INFY BDE

170TH MACHINE GUN COY.
FEB 1917 - FEB 1918.

57TH DIVISION
170TH INFY BDE

From O.C. 170 Machine Gun Company

To. O. C. 3rd Echelon
         Base

H517

Reference fm 140/457 dated 8.4.17.

I regret that the Nom. Rolls for
February of my Company were not
forwarded at the proper time.
The reason for this was that the
O.C. Sergeant and Sergt in Command
were both taken ill, and that down
the time of the same time, so that
the matter was overlooked.
Nom Rolls for March and
April were submitted at the proper
time.

I will see that it does
not occur again.

[signature]
for
O.C. 170 M. G. COY.

ORDERLY ROOM
Reference No. I.H.
Date
170 M.G COY.

57

WAR DIARY of 170 Machine Gun Company
or INTELLIGENCE SUMMARY. In the Field. FEBRUARY. 1917.

Vol I

Army Form C. 2118.

Place	Date	Hour	Summary of Events and Information	Remarks and references to Appendices
	9.2.17		Left Grantham 9.30 p.m.	
	10.2.17		Arrived Southampton. 6.20.a.m. Departed 5.30 p.m.	
	11.2.17		Arrived Havre, 1.15 a.m. per La Marguerite and Archimedes at 11 a.m.	
			Marched to No 2 Camp. Arrived No 2 Rest Camp 11 a.m. and 10.p.m.	
	12.2.17		Stood by in Camp.	
	13.2.17		Left Rest Camp. Two parties, transport and half Company. First party	
			left at 6.45 a.m. and entrained at 11. a.m. Second party at 10.15 a.m.	
			and entrained at 3.20 p.m.	
	14.2.17		In train.	
	15.2.17		Detrained at Bailleul. First party at 6.30 a.m. Second party 7.30 a.m.	
	16.2.17		In Billets.	
	17.2.17		Advance party reconnoitred trenches.	
	18.2.17		Left Billets at Bailleul. Company by motor lorry through	
	"		Armentières and Sailly over la-Lys to Cordonnerie Sector.	
	"		Transport came viâ Près Berquin and Sailly sur la Lys.	
	"		Relieved 3rd Company N. Z. M. G. Corpt. Relief complete at 9.30 p.m.	

Army Form C. 2118.

WAR DIARY
or
INTELLIGENCE SUMMARY.
(Erase heading not required.)

Instructions regarding War Diaries and Intelligence Summaries are contained in F. S. Regs., Part II. and the Staff Manual respectively. Title pages will be prepared in manuscript.

Place	Date	Hour	Summary of Events and Information	Remarks and references to Appendices
CORDONNERIE SECTOR	18.2.17		Disposition of Sections. No.1 and 2 Sections in front line. No. 3 Section at Indirect Billet. No. 4 Section at Company Headquarters.	
"	"		Situation normal.	
"	19.2.17		Very quiet.	
"	20.2.17		No. 4 Gun fired 750 rounds at Cross Roads, N.23.a.30.20 and N.22.d.95.85	
"	21.2.17		250 rounds fired from No. 3 Gun at German trenches. Wind Right.	
"	"		No. 5 Gun fired 1,000 rounds at Suspected dump N.22.a.80.70 and at trench N.22.a.50.50. to N.22.c.85.90. No. 6 Gun fired 500 rounds at roadway N.23.a.20.40 to N.23.a.30.20.	
"	22.2.17		2,000 rounds fired from two Support Guns on right at Cross Roads and Ammunition dump. One Support Gun on left fired at Cross Roads and searched Lane at N.11.d.40.60.	
"	"		Wind S.O.S.F. Two Guns fired 750 rounds from Indirect Billet at N.5.c. 4,500 rounds fired from Guns in Support line at Cross Roads, N.22.a.50.40 and N.22.c.80.90 and Rayon Track.	
"	23.2.17			
"	"			
"	24.2.17			
"	"			
"	25.2.17		Wind N.W. Four Guns fired 2,500 rounds at N.21.b.20.15. (Franklin)	

Army Form C. 2118.

WAR DIARY
or
INTELLIGENCE SUMMARY.
(Erase heading not required.)

Place	Date	Hour	Summary of Events and Information	Remarks and references to Appendices
CORDONNERIE SECTOR	25.2.17 (cont)		N 20 b 25.40 (House) N 22 d 80.60 (House) and N 22 b 90.55 (Cross Roads)	
"	26.2.17		Disposition of Sections. No.3 relieved No.2 Section on right. No.4 Section relieved No.1 on left. No.2 Section at Indirect Billet. No.1 Section in reserve at Company Headquarters.	
"			Short enemy bombardment on Cellar Farm Avenue.	
"	27.2.17		250 rounds fired at La Pelie M.20.b.30.50.	
"	28.2.17		Two Guns fired 1,250 rounds on track N 21 d and Leclercq Farm.	
"			1000 rounds were fired at N 22 b 90.00 and N 23 a 30.20.	

From O.C. 170 Machine Gun Company
To. D.A.G. 3rd Echelon

In compliance with G.R.O. 1598.
Herewith War Diary of the 170th Machine Gun Company, In the Field, for Month ending 31.3.17.

John A Barraclough
Lieut.
O.C. 170 M.G. COY.

Army Form C. 2118.

WAR DIARY
or
INTELLIGENCE SUMMARY
(Erase heading not required.)

170 Machine Gun Company
MARCH 1917

Place	Date	Hour	Summary of Events and Information	Remarks and references to Appendices
CORDONNERIE SECTOR	1/3/17		Company relieved by 173 M. G. Coy and proceeded to Rest Billets at Sailly-sur-la-Lys.	
SAILLY	2/3/17		General cleaning of Company Material and Limbers.	
SAILLY	3/3/17		Preparations for return to trenches.	
CORDONNERIE SECTOR	4/3/17		Relieved 173 M. G. Coy. Section I at Coy H'qrs Section II at Indirect Burst Section III Right Sector. Section IV Left Sector.	
"	5/3/17		Disposition of Sections the same. 500 rounds fired by Right Support gun on to HOYON TRACK.	
"	6/3/17		Disposition of Sections the same. 250 rounds fired on to HOYON TRACK. 1000 on to LE PIETRE.	
"	7/3/17		Disposition of Sections the same. 500 rounds fired on to LE PIETRE. 1500 on to suspected Dump at N.22.D.80.60.	
"	8/3/17		Disposition of Sections the same. 1000 rounds fired at FROMELLES FORK ROAD. N.22.B.80.40.	
"	9/3/17		Inter Company Relief :- No.1. Section to Left Sector. No.2. Section & Right Sector. No. 3. Section to Coy H'qrs. No.4 Section to Indirect Billet. LIEUT. CRAWFORD recalled to unit in England. 1500 rounds fired on HOYON TRACK. 1250 on LECLERCQ FARM.	
"	10/3/17		Rearrangement of guns & all guns withdrawn from FRONT LINE. No.1 Section relieving No. 5, 6, 7, & 8 guns in Supports. No. 2 Section relieving No.4 Support Gun, with three in reserve at V.C. HOUSE. 2nd LIEUT BONNER arrived from base as TRANSPORT OFFICER.	
"	11/3/17		Disposition of Sections the same. 2nd LIEUT. ILLINGWORTH to Hospital. 1000 rounds fired at Dump at N.22.D.80.60 by No.7 Gun. 1700 rounds fired at FROMELLES by No.8 Gun. 1500 rounds fired at HAYEM by No. 4 Gun.	

Army Form C. 2118.

WAR DIARY or INTELLIGENCE SUMMARY

(Erase heading not required.)

170 Machine Gun Company

MARCH 1917

Place	Date	Hour	Summary of Events and Information	Remarks and references to Appendices
CORDONNERIE SECTOR	12/3/17		Disposition of Sections the same. 1000 rounds fired at CROSS ROADS at N.21.C.60.30. 1000 at TRAM JUNCTION at N.23.B.35.35. 1000 at CROSS ROADS at N.23.A.30.20.	
"	13/3/17		Disposition of Sections the same. LIEUT. SYKES to hospital.	
"	14/3/17		Disposition of Sections the same. CAPT LAW to hospital. 2000 rounds fired on HOYON TRACK	
"	15/3/17		LIEUT BARRACLOUGH took temporary command of Company. Disposition of Sections the same. 1000 rounds fired by No.1 Sun on 4 NAYEM ROAD.	
"	16/3/17		Disposition of Sections the same. 4500 rounds fired on L. TRAM WAY JUNCTIONS at N.11.D.15.55 and N.23.B.35.35, 12 NAYEM FORK ROADS and FROMELLES.	
"	17/3/17		Into Company Relief:- No.1 Section to Deluret Billet. No.2.Section to Headquarters. No.3. Section to V.P. House and No.4. Sun. No.4. Section to S.6.7.9.B. Suns. 2500 rounds fired on TRAMWAY JUNCTIONS at N.21.D.60.70 and N.21.B.35.15 and FARM DELANGRÉ.	
"	18/3/17		Disposition of Sections the same. 2nd LIEUT. DAVIES went to hospital.	
"	19/3/17		Disposition of Sections the same. 1000 rounds fired into C.T. at N.15.D.90.40.	
"	20/3/17		Disposition of Sections the same. 1000 rounds fired on JUNCTION of C.T. with road at FME DE LA MARLAQUE at N.17.B.37.81.	
"	21/3/17		Disposition of Sections the same. 1250 rounds fired onto LES CLOCHERS at N.16.C.78.90.	
"	22/3/17		Disposition of Sections the same. 1.O.R. Casualty. 1000 rounds fired on enemy parapet N.15.C.60.10.	
"	23/3/17		Disposition of Sections the same. 1000 rounds fired on LES CLOCHERS.	
"	24/3/17		Disposition of Sections the same. Arrangements made to place BARRAGE round German Front Line from N.10.C.30.20 to N.10.C.42.2B & corn pit trench.	

Army Form C. 2118.

WAR DIARY
or
INTELLIGENCE SUMMARY

(Erase heading not required.)

170 Machine Gun Company

MARCH. 1917.

Place	Date	Hour	Summary of Events and Information	Remarks and references to Appendices
CORDONNERIE SECTOR	25/3/17		Inter Company Relief. No.1. Section E & V.C. Hunts and No.4. Gun No.2 Section E.5.6.7. & 8 guns No.3. Section & Indirect Batt. No.4. Section to Coy Headquarters BARRAGE carried out by 7 guns at 3.15 A.M. 19,875 rounds fired	
"	26/3/17		Disposition of Sections the same. 1000 rounds fired onto Rue DELAVAL N.14.B.35.60	
"	27/3/17		Disposition of Sections the same 1000 rounds fired onto NOYON TRACK - N.16.C.40.90 & N.21.A.90.70	
"	28/3/17		Disposition of Sections the same 500 rounds fired by No.8 Support gun onto CROSS ROADS at N.22.B.92.50	
"	29/3/17		Disposition of sections the same. LIEUT. S.E. MOORE arrived at Coy Hdqrs from Base. 1500 rounds fired onto ROAD from N.16.D.65.05 to 22.A.05.45 and N.24.A.20.60	
"	30/3/17		Disposition of Sections the same. 1000 rounds fired on TRENCH AREA N.21.A.75.80 & N.21.A.75.97.	
"	31/3/17		Disposition of Sections the same. 2500 rounds fired on suspected "MINNIE" POSITION at N.16.A.90.80	

From O C 170 Machine Gun Company
To D.A.G 3rd Echelon.

1-5-17

In compliance with G.R.O 1598, herewith War Diary of the 170th Machine Gun Company, In the Field, for month ending 30.4.17.

H.B.Law Capt.
O. C. 170 M. G. COY.

WAR DIARY OF 110 MACHINE GUN COMPANY IN THE FIELD

Army Form C. 2118.

INTELLIGENCE SUMMARY
(Erase heading not required.)

APRIL 1917

Vol 35

Place	Date	Hour	Summary of Events and Information	Remarks and references to Appendices
CORDONNERIE SECTOR	1/4/17		Defensive section the same	
"	2/4/17		1500 Rounds fired from indirect Battery Target Crucifix Road N.16.a.9080 to N.16.a.5950	
"			Inter section relief	
"			No1 Section to Coy Hq	
"			2 " " indirect Battery	
"			3 " " indirect Battery	
"			Nos 5,6,7,8 emplacements in outpost line	
"			4 V.C. Huns and No 4 gun position and new position at the ∧ of V.C.	
"			Answers in the Support line	
"			New scheme of indirect gun in the Support Line submitted from right to left	
"			submitted to C.O.R. 110th Brigade and approved by him	
"	3/4/17		Defensive of Section the same	
"			Indirect fire extended slightly owing to desire in getting new barrels from D.A.D.O.S.	
"	4/4/17		Defensive of Section the same	
"			450 Rounds fired by No. 5 gun Target Fritzed roads in Aubers	
"	5/4/17		Defensive of Section the same	
"			2000 Rounds fired at HOYON X-roads N.16.d.35-65 also N.22.d.10-40 also FROMELLES	

Army Form C. 2118.

WAR DIARY
or
INTELLIGENCE SUMMARY

(Erase heading not required.)

Place	Date	Hour	Summary of Events and Information	Remarks and references to Appendices
CORDONNERIE	3/4/17		1 Rapnelie of section the same. 1500 Obs fired at X roads at LES CLOCHERS and FROMELLES	
SECTOR	4/4/17		do. 500 " " Trenches N10c 15-45. Lieut S.E. Moore	
"	8/4/17		slightly wounded in the thigh (Shrapnel)	
"	8/4/17		1 Rapnelie of section the same. 1500 Obs fired at fort roads FROMELLES and LES CLOCHERS	
			Lieut S.E. Moore returned to duty	
"	9/4/17		1 Rapnelie of section the same. 1000 Obs fired at LA BIETTE in N.1.b.	
"	10/4/17		Indian section relief M01 to left section. M01 to right section and V.C. HOUSE M03 to Coy Hq.	
			M04 to INDIRECT BILLET.	
			500 rounds fired on ROAD in N.24.A. 20.60.	
"	11/4/17		Dispositions of sections the same. 1000 rounds fired on FROMELLES FORK ROAD N.22.6.90.55	
"	12/4/17		Dispositions of sections the same. 1500 rounds fired on Cross Roads at at DUMPS at	
			N.22.c.00.01. and N.10.d.15.20.	
"	13/4/17		Dispositions of section the same. 1500 rounds fired on Cross Roads at N.23.a. 30.20	
			FROMELLES and N.17.a.80.60.	
"	14/4/7		CAPT. ARKLE F.M. and 2nd LT. WOODWARD S.A. joined Company from Base. the former as O.C.	
			Coy. Dispositions of sections the same. 2000 rounds fired at FROMELLES FORK ROAD at	
			N.22.6.90.55 and the HAY in FORK ROAD.	

Army Form C. 2118.

WAR DIARY
or
INTELLIGENCE SUMMARY.
(Erase heading not required.)

Instructions regarding War Diaries and Intelligence Summaries are contained in F. S. Regs., Part II. and the Staff Manual respectively. Title pages will be prepared in manuscript.

Place	Date	Hour	Summary of Events and Information	Remarks and references to Appendices
CORDONNERIE SECTOR	15/4/17		Disposition of Sections the same. No.3. Section w/h Lts Moore and Wood H booked proceeded to ARMENTIERES in order to construct 4 Indirect Fire Emplacements during the night 15-16th in order to help form a machine gun Barrage for proposed raid on 36.I.26.c.72.08 & 26.c.95.20. 2,000 rounds fired on ROAD JUNCTION at N.24.a.20.60 and HAYEM FORK ROAD N.16.d.40.60.	
"	16/4/17		Disposition of Sections the same. 2 Lt O.W. DAVIES returned from sick leave. 2,000 rounds fired on ROAD JUNCTION at N.21.C.05.30 and WORKING PARTY observed at N.16.C.10.15.	
"	17/4/17		Disposition of Sections the same. Between 3.20 A.M and 3.45 A.M 11,000 rounds were fired by No.3. Section to support RAID in I.36.C. 1500 rounds fired on ROAD JUNCTION at N.21.C.05.30.	
"	18/4/17		Inter-Section Relief. No.1. Section at Indirect Billet No.2. Section at Coy H.qrs. No.3. Section at V.C. House and Right Section. No.4. Section in Support Line. 2,000 rounds fired on CRUCIFIX ROAD at N.16.a.39.41 & N.22.a.90.41. No.63959 Pte BLANCHARD H. warned by O.C. for want partial in charge of leaving his post whilst on Sentry Duty in Trenches.	
"	19/4/17		Disposition of Sections the same. 9,750 rounds fired on :- (1) TRACK from N.22.d.60.42 & N.12.d.20.95. (2) LECLERCQ FARM N.17.b.72.36. (3) REPORTED DUMP N.15.C.70.40 (4) HAYEM CROSS ROADS at N.16.d.38.60. (5) REPORTED DUMP? in WOOD at N.15.C.70.40 & N.15.d.10.30.	

Army Form C. 2118.

WAR DIARY
or
INTELLIGENCE SUMMARY.
(Erase heading not required.)

Instructions regarding War Diaries and Intelligence Summaries are contained in F. S. Regs., Part II. and the Staff Manual respectively. Title pages will be prepared in manuscript.

Place	Date	Hour	Summary of Events and Information	Remarks and references to Appendices
CORDONNERIE SECTOR	20/4/17		Disposition of Sections the same. Pte BLANCHARD tried by Court Martial (Man) Drunk, and sentenced to one year's imprisonment. Capt. H. B. LAW returned from sick leave. 7000 round's fired on :- (1) JUNCTION of C.T.s at LES CLOCHERS N.17.a.00.60 & N.16.b.70.35. (2) X. ROADS at HAYEM at N.16.A.38.60. (3) C.T.s and SUPPORTS N.16.b.00.45 & N.16.b.70.20. (4) X. ROADS FROMELLES N.22.6.90.35.	
"	21/4/17		Disposition of Sections the same. Capt. H.B. LAW took over Command of Coy from Capt. F. M. ARKLE. 6,750 rounds fired on (1) NEW SHEDS at N.15.6.05.70 (2) WORKING PARTY at N.16.C.20.10. (3) X. ROADS HAYEM at N.16.A.38.60 (4) C.T. at LES CLOCHERS N.17.A.00.60 & N.16.6.70.70.	
"	22/4/17		Disposition of Sections the same. 8,500 rounds fired at :- (1) NEW SHEDS at N.15.6.05.70 (2) LE CLERCQ FARM (3) X ROADS at HAYEM N.16.A.38.60.	
"	23/4/17		Disposition of Sections the same. 2.LT. WOODWARD G.A. transferred to 171 M.G. Coy. Scheme prepared and submitted to Brigade and Division for defence of CORDONNERIE - BOUTILLERIE SECTOR.	
CORDONNERIE	24/4/17		BOUTILLERIE SECTOR taken over from 171 M.G. Coy. New Disposition of Sections.	
BOUTILLERIE SECTOR	"		No.1. Section. 2 Guns in HUDSON BAY POST 1 Gun at SPY FARM 1 gun at BELTON LODGE.	
"	"		No 2 Section. Coy. HDQRS.	
"	"		No.3. Section. RIGHT SECTOR.	
"	"		No.4. Section. LEFT. SECTOR.	

WAR DIARY
or
INTELLIGENCE SUMMARY.

Army Form C. 2118.

(Erase heading not required.)

Place	Date	Hour	Summary of Events and Information	Remarks and references to Appendices
CORDONNERIE-BOU- TILLERIE SECTOR	25/4/17		Disposition of Sections the same. CAPT. F.M. ARKLE returned to the Base. No. 58671 PTE. EGGINGTON. F. remanded for F.G.C.M. on charge of wounding a comrade. Heavy M.G. fire. 1500 rounds fired from BELTON LODGE N.35.b.30.35 and SPY FARM b/.34.b.35.35. m N.11.d.50.80. and O.7.C.20.75.	
"	26/4/17		Disposition of Sections the same. 2000 rounds fired from BELTON LODGE and SPY FARM on N.12.d. 85.50 and b N.12.d.95.21 and N.13.a.00.15 & N.12.a.15.30.	
"	27/4/17.		Disposition of Sections the same. 2 LT. WOODWARD G.A. transferred back from 171 M.G. Coy. 3000 rds fired at N12.a.50-50 to NH.a.15-70 and N12.a.85.20 to N12.a 95-42.	
"	29/4/17		The Berlin relief No 1 section remained at Spy House and 9 and 10 sections in 2 Mons Lane No 2 Section to 5,6,7,8 mins Colthan Lane i.e. Centre under No. 5 section remained in 1, 2, 3 and 4 mines in Pitchard Pd. i.e. Right Sector. Nos 11 + 12 sections to Coy. Hqs. Lts. C.B. Booke & won the arrangements from the Line and retired to Mo. 3 section as reclives officers. 3250 Rds fired at N.11.d. 25-60 to N.11.d. 20-15 and N.11.d. 55-80 to N.11.d. 95-42.	
"	29		Disposition of sections the same. 2nd LT. T.B. Barron proceeded to SAMIERS for nephew for Coy. Lt. St. Johnson resume the comp. from 171 Coy. and is deposited to No 3 section. All seclres. officers. 4500 rds fired at N.11.d.55.02 to N.11.d.50-60 to N.11.d.80-80	

Army Form C. 2118.

WAR DIARY
or
INTELLIGENCE SUMMARY.
(Erase heading not required.)

Instructions regarding War Diaries and Intelligence Summaries are contained in F. S. Regs., Part II. and the Staff Manual respectively. Title pages will be prepared in manuscript.

Place	Date	Hour	Summary of Events and Information	Remarks and references to Appendices
CORDONNERIE	29.4.19		52611 Dr Egmidio J. tried by F.G.C.M. and sentenced to twenty informment with hard labour	
BOUTILLERIE	30.4.19		Disposition of Sections the same. 2000 rounds fired at N.11.d 20.60 to	
SECTOR			N.11.d 28.15 and N.12.d 95.80 to N.12.d 95.42	

Original

WAR DIARY OF 170 MACHINE GUN COMPANY.
FOR MAY, 1917.

INTELLIGENCE SUMMARY.

Vol 4

Army Form C. 2118.

Place	Date	Hour	Summary of Events and Information	Remarks and references to Appendices
CORDONERRIE – BOUTILLERIE SECTOR.	1-5-17		The line held by the Company is divided into three sectors. Right, Centre and Left. Distribution of sections. No 1. Left Sector. No 2. Centre Sector. No 3. Right Sector. No 4. Company Headquarters.	
"	2.5.17		1,500 rounds fired at CHATEAU RICHE N11d 50.40. Situation normal. 2,000 rounds fired at CHATEAU RICHE. N11d 50.40.	
"	3.5.17		Situation normal. 1,000 rounds fired at KEEPER'S COTTAGE, O7c 15.80. 1,000 rounds fired at ROAD N11d 15.60 to N11d 25.45. 24,000 rounds expended on Special barrage on ROAD from N16a 40.50 to N16a 80.50 to N16b 15.60 to N16b 40.60. Barrage ordered by 57½ Division owing to movement of troops observed during the day in back areas.	
"	4.5.17		Situation normal. The following targets were engaged owing to movement having been observed during the day. LES CLOCHERS, CROSS ROADS. NEGATIVE AVENUE. CHATEAU RICHE. N11d 85.60 to N12d 82.80. N12d 82.80 to N12d 95.42.	
"	5.5.17		Section relief. No 1 to Company Headquarters. No 2 to Centre Sector. No 3 to	

Army Form C. 2118.

WAR DIARY
or
INTELLIGENCE SUMMARY.
(Erase heading not required.)

Instructions regarding War Diaries and Intelligence Summaries are contained in F. S. Regs., Part II. and the Staff Manual respectively. Title pages will be prepared in manuscript.

Place	Date	Hour	Summary of Events and Information	Remarks and references to Appendices
CORDONNERIE -	5.5.17		Right Sector. No 4 to left Sector. No firing done owing to strong wind	
BOUTILLERIE	6.5.17		Situation normal. 1500 rounds fired at N12 a 20.30.	
SECTOR -	7.5.17		Situation normal. 1,500 rounds fired at N12 a 20.30.	
"	8.5.17		Situation normal. No firing. Company Headquarters called MARTYN LODGE.	
"	9.5.17		Situation normal. 2000 rounds at N11 d 20.56 to N11 b 30.00. and N11 d 98.40.	
"	10.5.17		Situation normal. 1,000 rounds at CHATEAU RICHE.	
"	11.5.17		Situation normal. 2,000 rounds at SUSPECTED DUMP at N12 a 40.05. and OLGA LANE. N12 b 55.18 to N12 d 96.40.	
"	12.5.17		Situation normal. 2000 rounds at N12 b. NEBULA SWITCH, N11 a. NED Roward. NED ALLEY.	
"	"		Sector relief. No 4 relieves No 3 Right Sector. No 2 Centre Sector. No 3 Martyn Lodge. No 4. Left Sector.	
"	13.5.17		Situation normal. 2,000 rounds at CHATEAU RICHE and road from NEBULA ALLEY to BAS MAISNIL.	
"	14.5.17		Situation normal. 2,250 rounds at N10 d. 30.60 to N11 c 00.45.	
"	15.5.17		Situation normal. 2,000 rounds at N10 b 98.90 and O 7 c 22.45.	

Army Form C. 2118.

WAR DIARY
or
INTELLIGENCE SUMMARY.

(Erase heading not required.)

Instructions regarding War Diaries and Intelligence Summaries are contained in F. S. Regs., Part II. and the Staff Manual respectively. Title pages will be prepared in manuscript.

Place	Date	Hour	Summary of Events and Information	Remarks and references to Appendices
CORDONNERIE	16.5.19		Situation normal. 1500 rounds at N16 b.70.78 and H12.c.	
BOUTILLERIE	17.5.19		" 2,000 rounds at RUE DES TURCS and NECK DRIVE.	
SECTOR	18.5.19		" 2,500 rounds from H34 b.49.19 and H35 b.80.40 at BAS MAISNIL and CHATEAU RICHE ROAD. N12.a.b.	
"	19.5.19		Inter section relief. No 1 Section at Right Section, No 2 Section at Company Headquarters, No 3 Section at Centre Section, No 4 Section at Left Section.	
"	"		2,000 rounds on CHATEAU RICHE and BAS MAISNIL ROAD. N12.a and b and NED ROW and NED ALLEY N11 a.c. from H34 b.49.19 and H35 b.80.40. 2,500 rounds special barrage from Indirect Billet and neighbourhood (1) N2 d 82.85 on N14 c 45.12 (2) N3 a 25.10 on N14 b 59.09 (3) N3 a 60.56 on N14 d 88.53. (4) N3 a 89.54. on FME DELAPORTE. N15.a. in connection with Infantry Raid.	
"	20.5.19		Situation normal. 1,500 rounds fired on O.Y.C. 25.90° from H34 b.49.19	
"	21.5.19		Situation normal. 1,450 rounds fired at BAS-MAISNIL and CHATEAU RICHE ROAD N12 a from H34 b.49.19 and H35 b.80.40. 500 rounds fired from same positions along enemy front line in support of Infantry raid.	

Army Form C. 2118.

WAR DIARY
INTELLIGENCE SUMMARY.
(Erase heading not required.)

Instructions regarding War Diaries and Intelligence Summaries are contained in F. S. Regs., Part II. and the Staff Manual respectively. Title pages will be prepared in manuscript.

Place	Date	Hour	Summary of Events and Information	Remarks and references to Appendices
CORDONNERIE - BOUTILLERIE SECTOR.	22.5.19		Situation normal. 2,500 rounds fired from H.34.b.49.19. and H.35.b.80.40 at BAS MAISNIL and CHATEAU RICHE ROAD. N.12.a. and NEBULA LODGE SWITCH. N.12.b. 1 O/Rank wounded by whizz-bang on both high.	
"	23.5.19		Situation normal. 3,500 rounds fired at BAS MAISNIL and CHATEAU RICHE ROAD. N.12.a. from H.34.b.49.19 and H.35.b.80.40. 500 rounds fired from N.5.b.62.53 in supports at Aeroplane.	
"	24.5.19		Situation normal. 2,000 rounds fired at CHATEAU RICHE and BAS MAISNIL ROAD N.12.a. from H.34.b.49.19 and H.35.b.80.40. 400 rounds fired at Aeroplane.	
"	25.5.19		Situation normal. 1,000 rounds fired from H.34.b.49.19. on NEBULA SWITCH. N.12.a. 1,000 rounds fired from H.35.b.80.40 at NED ROW N.11.a. Inter section relief. No 1 Section at V.C. HOUSE and Right Sector. No 2 Section at SPY FARM and Left Sector. No 3 Section at Centre Sector and No 4 Section at Company Headquarters.	
"	26.5.19		1,500 rounds fired from H.34.b.49.19 on NED NECK and NEBULA, N.11.a.b.12.a. KEEPER'S COTTAGE O.y.c. 15.45. ROAD at N.12.a. 15.20.	

Army Form C. 2118.

WAR DIARY
or
INTELLIGENCE SUMMARY.

(Erase heading not required.)

Instructions regarding War Diaries and Intelligence Summaries are contained in F. S. Regs., Part II. and the Staff Manual respectively. Title pages will be prepared in manuscript.

Place	Date	Hour	Summary of Events and Information	Remarks and references to Appendices
CORDONNERIE	27.5.19		1,500 rounds fired from H.35.b.80.40 on CHATEAU RICHE ROAD N.12.a.	
BOUTILLERIE	28.5.19		Situation normal. 2,000 rounds fired from H.34.b.49.19 and H.35.b.80.40 on CHATEAU RICHE - BAS MAISNIL ROAD. N.12.a and NECK and NEBULA H.11 and 12a	
SECTOR	29.5.19		Situation normal. 2,500 rounds fired from H.34.b.49.19 and H.35.b.80.40 on CHATEAU RICHE and BAS-MAISNIL ROAD N.12.a and NECK and NEBULA. N.11.b and 12.a.	
"	"			
"	30.5.19		Situation normal. 2,000 rounds fired from H.34.d.49.19 and N.12.a.95.50 and NEBULA POINT and from H.35.b.80.40 on CHATEAU RICHE & NEBULA ALLEY N.11.d and 12.a.	
"	31.5.19		Situation normal. 2,000 rounds fired from H.34.b.49.19 and H.35.b.80.40 at CHATEAU RICHE N.11.d.50.% and NEBULA SWITCH N.12.b. One Plant slightly gassed.	

From O.C. 170 Machine Gun Company
To Headquarters, 57th Division.

July 1st 1917.

In compliance with G.R.O. No. 1598, herewith War Diary of the 170th Machine Gun Company for the month of June 1917.

H B Laws Capt.
O.C. 170 M.G. COY.

Army Form C. 2118.

WAR DIARY OF 170 MACHINE GUN COY.

INTELLIGENCE SUMMARY

IN THE FIELD. **JUNE 1917.**

(Erase heading not required.)

Vol 5

Place	Date	Hour	Summary of Events and Information	Remarks and references to Appendices
	JUNE			
CORDONNERIE —	1ST		Situation normal. 750 rounds fired from H.34.b.4.9.19. on CHATEAU RICHE —	
BOUTILLERIE			BAS MAISNIL ROAD. 750 rounds fired from H.35.b.80.40. on N12.a.60.58. MINNIE	
SECTOR.			EMPLACEMENT.	
"	2ND		Section relief. No.1 Section at Company Headquarters. No.2 Section at	
"			SPY FARM. No.3 Section at CENTRE SECTOR. No.4 Section at RIGHT SECTOR.	
"			1500 rounds fired from H.34.b.4.9.19 and H.35.b.80.40. on to N12.a.60.58	
"			MINNIE EMPLACEMENT and CHATEAU RICHE — BAS MAISNIL ROAD.	
"	3RD		Situation normal. 1000 rounds fired at CHATEAU RICHE — BAS MAISNIL ROAD	
"			from H.34.b.4.9.19 and H.35.b.80.40. 250 rounds fired at Aeroplanes.	
"			No. 33333 Sgt. ROWLANDS. G.O. No. 58188 Pte BROWN. T. No. 55958 Pte HARVEY. W.	
"			No. 43965 Pte ARNOLD. H. were killed by same Shell at N.9.06.34.	
"			No. 50528 Pte BRANNON. C. was wounded and died later on the day.	
"	4TH		Situation normal. 1000 rounds fired from H.34.b.4.9.19 and	
"			H.35.b.80.40. on NED ROW. N12.a.10.22.	
"	5TH		Situation normal. 1000 rounds fired from H.34.b.4.9.19. and H.35.b.80.40.	
"			on NED ROW and NECK TRIV.	

Army Form C. 2118.

WAR DIARY
or
INTELLIGENCE SUMMARY.
(Erase heading not required.)

Place	Date	Hour	Summary of Events and Information	Remarks and references to Appendices
CORDONNERIE-BOUTILLERIE SECTOR.	6TH	-	Situation normal. 1,500 rounds fired from H.34.b.49.19. H.35.b.80.10 on M.G. Emp.	
"	7TH		PLACEMENT at N.12.d.4.3.48.	
"	8TH		Situation normal. 1,600 rounds fired from H.34.b.49.19 and H.35.b.80.40. at N.18.a.H.2.48. and NEBULA LANE.	
"	"		Situation normal. 3,000 rounds fired from (1) N.9.a.5.10.40 at HONEY TRENCH	
"	"		(2) N.9.b.05.34 at FARM PETRE. (3) H.34.b.49.19 at NECK LANE, NECK AVENUE.	
"	"		(4) H.35.b.80.40 at M.G. EMPLACEMENT at N.12.d.4.3.48.	
"	9TH		Sector relief. No.1 Section CENTRE SECTOR. No.2 LEFT SECTOR.	
"	"		No.3. COMPANY HEADQUARTERS. No.4. V.C. HOUSE.	
"	"		3,500 rounds fired from (1) N.8.a.70.40 at FROMELLES CROSS ROADS.	
"	"		(2) N.9.b.05.34 at C.T. N.20.d. (3) H.34.b.49.19 at CHATEAU RICHE — BAS	
"	"		MAISNIL ROAD. (4) H.35.b.80.40. at O.9.a.68.95.	
"	10TH		Situation normal. 2,000 rounds fired from. (1) N.9.b.05.35 at	
"	"		C.T. N.20.d. (2) H.34.b.49.19 at CHATEAU RICHE — BAS MAISNIL ROAD.	
"	"		(3) H.35.b.80.40. at KEEPER'S COTTAGE. N.12.c.00.85.	
"	11TH		Situation normal. 3,500 rounds fired from (1) H.34.b.49.19. at	

Army Form C. 2118.

WAR DIARY
or
INTELLIGENCE SUMMARY.
(Erase heading not required.)

Instructions regarding War Diaries and Intelligence Summaries are contained in F. S. Regs., Part II. and the Staff Manual respectively. Title pages will be prepared in manuscript.

Place	Date	Hour	Summary of Events and Information	Remarks and references to Appendices
CORDONNERIE- BOUTILLERIE SECTOR.	11th		CHATEAU RICHE DUMP. (2) N 8a 90.40. at TRAMWAY N 22 d 95.95. (3) N 9 c 05.34. at C.T. N 21 d.	
"	"		No. 6767 Pte. HARVEY. R.M. wounded by shell in HUDSON BAY. Died shortly after admittance to Hospital. Our just out of action by same shell.	
"	12th		Situation normal. 2,500 rounds fired from (1) N y 6- 92.36. at DUG- OUT N 22 c 30.10. (2) N 8 d 80.40. at CROSS ROADS. N 21 c 02-05. (3) H 34 6 49.19 at NECK ARNE.	
"	"		140th BRIGADE C.O. 40.36. received. Patrols to be formed in enemy front line in order to recce via closer touch and to show greater offensiveness.	
"	"		(1) BRIGHOUSE. N 9 c 40.10. (approx) (2) HALIFAX. N 9 d 65.18. (approx) (3) HULL N 10 d 40.55 (approx) (4) BOLTON. N 11 a 35.58.	
"	"		In order to bring M.G. protection, the following scheme observed:- (a) front line (1) X N 9 d 86.37. bringing a belt of fire in front of HALIFAX POST. (2) Y. N 9 c 40.45 bringing a belt of fire in front of BOLTON POST. (3) Z. N 5 d 60.84. bringing a belt of fire when the posts call for a S.O.S.	
"	"		The above guns only open fire when the posts call for a S.O.S.	

Army Form C. 2118.

WAR DIARY
or
INTELLIGENCE SUMMARY.
(Erase heading not required.)

Instructions regarding War Diaries and Intelligence Summaries are contained in F.S. Regs., Part II. and the Staff Manual respectively. Title pages will be prepared in manuscript.

Place	Date	Hour	Summary of Events and Information	Remarks and references to Appendices
CORDONNERIE BOUTILLERIE SECTOR	12th		(b) SUPPORT LINE. The following Guns in indirect fire positions to engage the following targets:-	
"	"		No.1 GUN. MAP REFERENCE. N8a.93.40. TARGET. CROSS ROADS at N21c.02.34.	
"	"		" 2 " " N8.85.50 " JUNCTION OF ROADS at N17b.30.72.	
"	"		" 3 " " N4d.33.38. " JUNCTION OF TRENCHES at N23a.50.95	
"	"		The above mentioned Guns will fire short bursts of covering fire during the operation from ZERO hour onwards.	
"	"		(c) Guns in indirect Fire Positions between SUPPORT LINE and RUE DU BOIS, will engage targets as below:-	
"	"		Guns Map Reference. Target. Map Reference	
"	"		A. N2d.81.83 Fme DELANGRE N10d.08.25.	
"	"		B. N3a.25.10. " "	
"	"		C. N3a.60.56. HOUSE at. N14d.78.53.	
"	"		C1. N3a.83.51. ROAD JUNCTION at. N16d.26.60.	
"	"		C and C1. to fire short bursts to cover advance of Infantry from Zero hour onwards. A and B only to fire if S.O.S. call goes up.	

WAR DIARY or INTELLIGENCE SUMMARY.

Army Form C. 2118.

(Erase heading not required.)

Place	Date	Hour	Summary of Events and Information	Remarks and references to Appendices
CORDONNERIE BOUTILLERIE SECTOR	12TH		Two guns to be placed in the Brigade on right.	
"	"		GUN. MAP REFERENCE. TARGET. MAP REFERENCE	
"	"		V. M12d. 22.10. FME DELAPORTE (To cover Brigmouse) N15a 75.60.	
"	"		W. M12d. 20.00. HOUSE AT (To cover Hollifax) N15b 75.65.	
"	"		These guns to fire short bursts at intervals from ZERO HOUR onwards to cover advance of Infantry and to be available in case of an S.O.S. Situation normal. 2,500 fired from (1)N34b6 49.19. at NECK DRIVE.	
"	13TH		(2) N9b 82.36 at Aug-out. N22c. (3) N9b 05.34. at FROMELLES CROSS ROADS. N22b 90.64	
"	"		Situation normal. 3,500 rounds fired from (1)N9b 92.36 at FROMELLES CROSS ROADS N22b 91.60. (3)N9b 05.34 at TRAMLINE N22c 50.20 @N8a 50.40	
"	14TH		at TRENCH N21b 75.40 (4)H34b 49.19. at CHATEAU RICHE.	
"	"		2 Officers and 68 O/Ranks with 1 guns returned from 199 M.G. Coy. to assist in proposed operations, paid for nights shine 15/16. Gun positions chosen and constructed. Shelter and Dug-outs cleared	
"	"		or constructed at X Y Z.	

WAR DIARY
or
INTELLIGENCE SUMMARY

Army Form C. 2118.

Place	Date	Hour	Summary of Events and Information	Remarks and references to Appendices
CORDONNERIE BOUTILLERIE SECTOR	15TH		Situation normal. 1,500 rounds fired from (1) N9b 05.34 at N14t 60.30.	
"	"		(2) H34 t 49.19 at TRENCH N18 a 45.80 to N13c 4.80.	
"	"		H.Q. a/c Overhead hopposed in Brigade O.O. to 36 indefinitely postponed.	
"	16TH		Officers, men and guns from 199 M.G. Coy returned to 1st B.F.S. Section relief. No 1 Section at Centre Sector.	
"	"		No 2. at Company Headquarters No 3. at Left Sector and Spy Farm.	
"	"		No 4 Section at Right Sector. V. C. Kennel.	
"	"		3,000 rounds fired from (1) H34 t 49.19 at BAS MAISNIL ROAD. (2) N9t 82.36 at KERT N.23 a 00.40 to N.23 c 22.30. (3) NR a 50.40 at Junction of C.T. and Road at N.25 t 89.90.	
"	17TH		Situation normal. 2,000 rounds fired from (1) H34 t 49.19 on BAS MAISNIL ROAD. (2) H35 t 80.40 on OLGA LANE N12 t 63.14 - N12 d 93.62.	
"	18TH		Situation normal. 2000 rounds fired from H34 t 49.19 on BAS MAISNIL ROAD. (2) H35 t 80.40 at "MARTIN'S CORNER" O9 a 95.60.	
"	19TH		Situation normal. 3,500 rounds fired from (1) N9t 82.36 at M.G. EMPLACEMENT. N30 c 20.55. (2) H34 t 49.19 at TRAMLINE N12 a 55.25 to	

WAR DIARY
or
INTELLIGENCE SUMMARY

Army Form C. 2118.

Place	Date	Hour	Summary of Events and Information	Remarks and references to Appendices
CORDONNERIE BOUTILLERIE SECTOR	19		N12.c.1080 and N.12.c.2080. Instructions issued to prepare again for Bujak O.P 1896.	
"	20		Situation normal. 6000 rounds fired from (1)N.N.c.a 6c.40 at N12.c.050- (2)N.g.b.05.37 at N.22.A.05.90 (3)H.34.b.49.17 at WORKING PARTY at N.12.c.2080 (4) N.34.60.56 at CROSS ROADS, HAYEM, N.b.d.35.60 (5)H.35 + 2040 at MARTIN'S CORNER 07 a 2560 (6) N.3.a.25.10 at HOUSE at N.14.d.55.55	
"	21st		Situation normal. 2000 rounds fired from (1) H.34.b.49.17 at 1345 MAISNIL ROAD, N.12.b.05.50 (2) H.35.A.50.40 at ST N.12.a.40.05 to N.12.c.51.82	
"	"		Officer 26 0/Hs went to inns reported from 16th Motor Machine Gun Battery to aid in carrying out scheme outlined in Brigade O.O No 36. 2 km had received a footjourney Bde O.O. 36 instructing 16th M.M.G. Battery to gives advice to, to gives	
"	"		CORPS RESERVE	
"	22		Situation normal. 2000 rounds fired from (1) H34.b.49.17 at CHATEAU RICHE N.12.c.15.75 (2) H.35.+.2040 at WORKING PARTY in C.T. near Section Relief. No.1 Section in Centre Sector No.2 Section	

WAR DIARY or INTELLIGENCE SUMMARY

Army Form C. 2118.

(Erase heading not required.)

Instructions regarding War Diaries and Intelligence Summaries are contained in F. S. Regs., Part II and the Staff Manual respectively. Title pages will be prepared in manuscript.

Place	Date	Hour	Summary of Events and Information	Remarks and references to Appendices
BoisDunnerie-Bouillerie Section	23rd		M Right Centre (V.C. House) No 3 Section Left Sector (Spy Farm). No 4 Section at Company Headquarters.	
"	"		2000 rounds fired from (1) H.34.b.25.38 at BAS MAISNIL ROAD, N.12.b.05.65 (2) H.35.b.30.34 at new C.T. in course of construction N.12.c.25.80	
"	24		Situation normal. Lieut. J.E. Moore left for Base.	
"	"		2000 rounds fired from (1) H.35.b.30.34 at N.12.d.45.80 to N.18.a.40.15 (2) N.9.b.25.30 at ROAD N.22.b.90.60 to N.23.a.30.20	
"	25th		Situation normal. 2250 rounds fired from (1) H.34.b.25.38 at N.12.a 54.34, JUNCTION of TRENCHES and BAS MAISNIL ROAD (2) H.35.b.30.34 at Trench N.12.d.50.80 to N.18.a.44.78 (3) N.8.a.73.46 at N.21.c.05.25 CROSS ROADS.	
"	26		Situation normal. 2000 rounds fired from (1) N.9.A.47.36 at N.21.b.25.09 (2) H.34.b.25.38 at OLGA LANE (3) H.35.b.30.34 at CHATEAU RICHE and BAS MAISNIL ROAD.	
"	27		Situation normal. 2500 rounds fired from (1) H.35.b.30.34 at TRENCH N.12.d.25.60 to N.18.a.43.78 (2) H.34.b.25.38 at CHATEAU RICHE- BAS MAISNIL ROAD	

Army Form C. 2118.

WAR DIARY
or
INTELLIGENCE SUMMARY.
(Erase heading not required.)

Instructions regarding War Diaries and Intelligence Summaries are contained in F. S. Regs., Part II. and the Staff Manual respectively. Title pages will be prepared in manuscript.

Place	Date	Hour	Summary of Events and Information	Remarks and references to Appendices
CORDONNERIE-BOUTILLERIE SECTOR	27		(3) N.9.c.25.30. at FRIE DU MOYON N.22.d.1.65	
"	28		Situation normal. 2500 rounds fired from (1) N.8.c.71.40 at N.11.C.03.25	
"			(2) H.35.b.30.34 at TRENCH N.12.a.35.60 to N.18.a.45.78 (3) H.34.b.25.38 at CHATEAU RICHE BAS MAISNIL ROAD. 1250 rounds fired from Support Line at aeroplanes. Owing to increased aa activity Anti-aircraft positions established within 150 yds of Nos. 2, 4, 5, 7, 7 gun positions in Support Line	
"	29		Situation normal. 200 rounds fired from (1) H.35.b.30.34 at INDEX AVENUE. (2) N.9.c.92.36 at N.23.c.40.20. support dump.	
"	30		Section relief. No 1. Section at Company Headquarters No 2 Section in Right Sector (V.C Avenue), No 3 Section in Left Sector (Apo Farm) No 4 Section in Centre Sector. 200 rounds fired from (1) H.35.b.30.34 on INDEX AVENUE (2) N.9.b.25.30. at N.22.c.65.50 Suspected Dump	

Instructions regarding War Diaries and Intelligence Summaries are contained in F.S. Regs., Part II. and the Staff Manual respectively. Title pages will be prepared in manuscript.

WAR DIARY OF 170 MACHINE GUN COY

Army Form C. 2118.

INTELLIGENCE SUMMARY

IN THE FIELD. JULY 1917

Vol 6

(Erase heading not required.)

Place	Date	Hour	Summary of Events and Information	Remarks and references to Appendices
CORDONNERIE - BOUTILLERIE SECTOR.	JULY 1st		(1) Situation normal. 2750 rounds fired from :- (1) H.34.t.25.38. at DUMP at N.12.a.60.48. and NEBULA SWITCH and INDEX AVENUE. (3) H.34.t.91.40 at SUSPECTED DUMP at N.8.7.10.15.	
	"	2nd	Situation normal 4000 rounds fired from :- (1) N.9.t.25.30 at N.22.c.50.30 and N.22.t.10.60. (2) H.34.t.25.38 at CHATEAU RICHE - BAS MAISNIL ROAD and DUMP at N.12.a.60.43. (3) H.35.t.30.34 at OLGA SWITCH and NECK DRIVE. (4) 4500 rounds fired from suspected at HOSTILE HAVES	
	"	3rd	Situation normal. 3000 rounds fired from :- N.9.t.92.34 at N.22.c.50.60. (2) H.34.t.25.38 at NEBULA SWITCH, AND DUMP AT N.12.a.60.50. (3) H.35.t.30.34 at OLGA SWITCH and NECK DRIVE.	
	"	4	Situation normal. 2000 yards fired from :- (1) H.34.t.25.38 at DUMP N.12.a.60.48. (2) H.35.t.30.34 at NEW TRENCH N.12.9000. TO N.13.1010.	
	"	5	Situation normal. 3000 rounds fired from (1) H.35.t.30.34 at INDEX AVE. MARTIN'S CORNER, KEEPER'S COTTAGE. (2) H.34.t.25.38 at NEBULA DRIVE, SWITCH NECK DRIVE and NED ROW. (3) N.9.t.92.36 at N.22.C.30.10. No. 53998. Pte. Foss L. was tried by F.G.C.M. on the following charge:-	

Army Form C. 2118.

WAR DIARY
or
INTELLIGENCE SUMMARY.
(Erase heading not required.)

Instructions regarding War Diaries and Intelligence Summaries are contained in F. S. Regs., Part II. and the Staff Manual respectively. Title pages will be prepared in manuscript.

Place	Date	Hour	Summary of Events and Information	Remarks and references to Appendices
CORDONNERIE BOUTILLERIE SECTOR	5th		Men on active service, conduct to the prejudice of good order and military discipline (negligently wounding himself) He was found guilty and sentenced to 15 days F.P. No.1.	
"	6th		Situation normal.	
"	7th		Situation normal. Section relief Agr. at SPY FARM, LEFT SECTOR No.2 RIGHT SECTOR, No.3 COMPANY HEADQUARTERS, No.4 CENTRE SECTOR 2500 rounds fired from - N.8.a.93.40. at N.16.c.10.15, (2) N.9.b.25.30 at N.21.c.05.25 (3) H.34.b.25.38 at ROAD FROM N.11.d.20.55. TO N.11.d.25.15.	
"	8th		Situation normal. 2500 rounds fired from - (1) H.35.b.25.38 at ROAD from N.12.d.80.80. to N.12.d.95.40 (2) N.8.a.93.40 at N.16.a.76.00 (3) N.9.b.25.30 at N.21.a.05.25	
"	9th		Situation normal. 2000 rounds fired from (1) N.9.b.93.36 at N.22.d.05.60. N.22.b.70.97, N.12.b.95.SH, (2) H.35.b.25.38 at TRENCH from N.12.c.30.40 to N.12.c.30.98.	
"	10th		Situation normal. 1750 rounds fired from (1) N.8.a.93.40 at CROSS ROADS at N.21.C.04.25 (2) H.35.b.25.30 at KEEPERS COTTAGE N.7.c.15.75	

Army Form C. 2118.

WAR DIARY
or
INTELLIGENCE SUMMARY.

(Erase heading not required.)

Place	Date	Hour	Summary of Events and Information	Remarks and references to Appendices
CORDONNERIE-BOUTILLERIE SECTOR	July 11th		Situation normal. 1000 rounds fired from H.35.b.25.38 at O.6.A SWITCH from N.12.C.90.15 to N.12.d.20.50.	
"	12		Situation normal. In connection with new Brigade Defence Scheme No 4 gun moved to N.10.a.40.52 (approx). 1000 rounds fired from H.35.b.25.38 to O.6.A SWITCH from N.12.c.90.15 to N.12.d.20.50.	
"	13		Situation normal. 4 Section of 17th M.G. Company ordered up to support the advance to assist in the advance party. Rail arranged for night of October July 14th. 2000 rounds fired from (1) H.35.d.30.4. ROAD from N.11.6.82.02 to N.11.a.14.20 (2) H.35.b.25.38 at ROAD N.6.a.70.80 to N.6.6.70.10. 100 rounds fired at aeroplane.	
"	14th		Situation normal. Section relief No 1 Section to Left Sector, No 2 to Coy Headquarters, No 3 to Right Sector, No 4 to Centre Sector. 500 rounds fired at aeroplane. Appendix 2. 170 Brigade Operation Order No 47 "Hartpoes Hunt". Number of guns to be used in all — 8. One to protect left flank and remainder for indirect fire.	

WAR DIARY
or
INTELLIGENCE SUMMARY

Army Form C. 2118.

Place	Date	Hour	Summary of Events and Information	Remarks and references to Appendices
CORDONNERIE - BOUTILLERIE SECTOR	14th		**TARGET.** **BEARINGS.**	
"	"		GUN.	
"	"		C. 2 N.3.a.60.56. DOLLS HOUSE, N.11.c.30.20. 130/5 T bearing.	
"	"		Cl. 2 N.3.a.63.57. CHATEAU RICHE, N.11.d.50.75. 120/5 T "	
"	"		1. 2 H.35.a.95.11. ROAD TO BE TRAVERSED FROM N.11.b.22.02. TO N.12.a.14.20. 164 T Centre bearing	
"	"		2. 2 H.35.b.05.15. ROAD TO BE TRAVERSED FROM N.12.a.14.20. TO N.12.a.46.35. 159 T "	
"	"		3. 2 H.35.b.16.22. ROAD TO BE TRAVERSED FROM N.12.a.46.35. TO N.12.a.70.48. 159 T "	
"	"		4. 2 H.34.b.25.38. TRENCH AT N.6.d.70.80. TRAVERSE TO N.6.9.76.99.	
"	"		5. 2 H.35.d.41.36. ROAD AT N.12.b.45.05. 153 T bearing.	
"	"		All the above guns will fire short bursts of fire during the evening of Zero day before Zero hour, and will continue to do this after Zero hour in order to cover the advance of the raiding party. They will not fire enough to become unduly suspicious. Indirect fire will be carried out on these targets for two or three days preceding Zero day. The gun to give protective fire if necessary on the left flank of the raid, will be posted at N.6.b.32.56. This gun will form the enemy's parapet, and will fire on a bearing of 197 T.	
"	"		The fire will be subject to orders from the O.C. Raid and will not	

WAR DIARY
or
INTELLIGENCE SUMMARY
(Erase heading not required.)

Army Form C. 2118.

Place	Date	Hour	Summary of Events and Information	Remarks and references to Appendices
CORDONNERIE - BOUTILLERIE SECTOR	July 14th		Fire unless Co thinks it necessary, except of course when the S.O.S. is given. In case the S.O.S. signal being given all guns will immediately open rapid fire and continue same for 3 minutes and then resume all ordinary rate of fire until told to do so by the M Lillers	
	15"		17,500 rounds fired in ordinary week shoot and Situation normal. 2 O.Rs admitted to Hospital suffering from bad poisoning due to sustained 15 enemy raid on premises at	
	16"		500 rounds fired at bombing. Section at 173 M.C. Leer reliance to hour Coy. Situation normal. 1000 rounds fired from H.35.b.25.38 at ROAD from N.12.d.50.50 to N.12.d.95.50.	
	17"		Situation normal. 1000 rounds fired from H.35.b.25.38 at OLGA SWITCH N.12.c.85.15 to N.12.d.20.50. 250 rounds from N.H.d.42.43 on F.L. testing limits of traverse.	
	18"		Situation normal. 500 rounds fired from H.35.b.32.38 at TRENCH N.6.4.90.70 to O.L.6.20.92. 250 rounds in registration on F.L.	

WAR DIARY
or
INTELLIGENCE SUMMARY

(Erase heading not required.)

Army Form C. 2118.

Place	Date	Hour	Summary of Events and Information	Remarks and references to Appendices
CORDONNERIE—BOUTILLERIE SECTOR	July 18		4 M.M.G's of 15th M.G. Battery arrived to help in opposition of "Harfords Hunt"	
"	19th		Situation normal. 1000 rounds fired from H.34.b.30.34 at NEBULA DRIVE and NEBULA SWITCH N.2.t.00.50 to N.12.b.15.30	
"	"		500 rounds fired on registration in F.L	
"	20th		Situation normal. Repetition of HARFORDS HUNT disposition of guns identical with that of July 14th 26,250 rounds fired in conjunction with raid. 550 rounds fired at Hawthorn.	
"	"		Situation normal. Section relief. No 1 Section to Left Sector, No 2 Section to Centre Sector, No 3 Section to Right Sector, No 4 Section at Company Headquarters.	
"	21st		Registration on front line in connection with rest Brigade Defence Scheme. 500 rounds.	
"	"		2,050 rounds fired from (1) N.8.a.92.40 at O.F.L. (2) N.8.b.55.50 at O.F.L. owing to S.O.S. signal	
"	22nd		Situation normal. 500 rounds fired from H.34.b.30.34 at	

Army Form C. 2118.

WAR DIARY
or
INTELLIGENCE SUMMARY.

(Erase heading not required.)

Instructions regarding War Diaries and Intelligence Summaries are contained in F. S. Regs., Part II. and the Staff Manual respectively. Title pages will be prepared in manuscript.

Place	Date	Hour	Summary of Events and Information	Remarks and references to Appendices
CORDONNERIE-BOUTILLERIE SECTOR	July 22		CHATEAU RICHE ROAD and NEPON AVENUE. 2200 rounds fired at hostile aeroplanes.	
"	23		Situation normal. 850 rounds fired from H.34.b.25.37 at KEEPERS	
			COTTAGE. 1100 rounds fired at hostile aeroplanes.	
"			1250 rounds fired in response to S.O.S.	
"	24		Situation normal. 1000 rounds fired from H.34.b.25.38 at	
			BAS MAISNIL, NEBULA AVENUE and SWITCH.	
"	25		Situation normal.	
"	26		Situation normal. 1500 rounds fired from H.34.b.25.37	
			N.11.c.90.60 to N.11.c.15.38.	
"			at CHATEAU RICHE ROAD.	
"	27		Situation normal. 5050 rounds fired in conjunction	
			with Bypass Operation Order No 52. 3 spots taken	
			(1) Numbers of same to be used	5
			Southwest line	3
			+ Tankin fire from front line	2
			(2)	

A6945 Wt. W11422/M1160 350,000 12/16 D. D. & L. Forms/C/2118/14

WAR DIARY or INTELLIGENCE SUMMARY

Army Form C. 2118.

Place	Date	Hour	Summary of Events and Information	Remarks and references to Appendices
CORDONNERIE - BOUTILLERIE SECTOR	JULY		B.O.O.1.0.57 (cont)	
"			(3) INDIRECT FIRE	
"			GUN MAP REFERENCE TARGET MAP REFERENCE	
"			C1 N.3.a.53.57. This gun will search trenches and cross roads from N.10.d.55.05 to N.16.b.94.23, and will also traverse from N.16.b.15.65 to N.10.d.55.07	
"			1 H.34.b.32.12. This gun will search NED AVENUE from N.11.c.63.27 to N.11.d.1820.	
"			2 (BELTON LODGE) H.35.b.2034 DOLLS HOUSE N11.c.3.30.	
"			(2) FLANKING FIRE	
"			A N.10.b.40.04 This gun will skim enemy parapet and will fire on a bearing of 155°T and will give protection fire to the right flank of 2 x u.t	
"			B N.10.b.75.05 This gun will skim enemy parapet and will fire on a bearing of 130½°T and will give protective fire for the left flank of battalion.	

WAR DIARY
or
INTELLIGENCE SUMMARY.
(Erase heading not required.)

Army Form C. 2118.

Place	Date	Hour	Summary of Events and Information	Remarks and references to Appendices
CONDONNERIE	JULY		Covering	
BOUILLERIE SECTOR	27		(4) No 2 gun will open short bursts of fire from Zero hour until the ranging parties have returned to our lines.	
			Guns C, 1, A, and B, will not fire at all unless our Artillery opens fire, in which case all guns will open rapid fire and continue same for 5 minutes. When they will naturally cease f. taking their cue from the Artillery.	
	28		(5) Situation normal. Section relief — No 1 Section at Company Headquarters No 2 Section in Centre Sector, No. 3 Section in Right Sector, No 4 Section in Left Sector.	
			2.00 Second part in accordance with Brigade Operation Order No 53 (from B gun position) as below:-	
			(1.) Number of guns to be used — 2 — indirect fire — flanking fire from front line —	
			Total 4 guns.	
			cont over	

WAR DIARY
or
INTELLIGENCE SUMMARY.

(Erase heading not required.)

Army Form C. 2118.

Place	Date	Hour	Summary of Events and Information	Remarks and references to Appendices
CORDONNERIE BOUTILLERIE SECTOR	July 26		(2) INDIRECT FIRE	
			GUN MAP REF. REMARKS	
	"		B. N.3.a.25.10. This gun will fire on LA BIETTE at:-	
	"		N.16.c.45.92. Also on trench at N.15.d.75.87	
	"		and will traverse from N.15.d.78.96 to	
	"		N.16.a.21.07., and from N.16.a.41.11 to	
	"		N.16.a.72.38.	
	"		C. N.3.a.61.56. This gun will search the road from	
	"		N.16.a.62.55 to N.16.a.27.66	
	"		(3) FLANKING FIRE	
	"		X N.9.c.54.80. This gun will strew the enemy's parapet and	
	"		will fire on a bearing of 157°T, so giving	
	"		protective fire for the right flank of the raid.	
	"		Y N.10.c.38.61. This gun will strew the enemy's parapet	
	"		and will fire on a bearing of 145°T, 30	
	"		giving protective fire for the left flank of the raid.	
			Cont.	

WAR DIARY
or
INTELLIGENCE SUMMARY.
(Erase heading not required.)

Army Form C. 2118.

Place	Date	Hour	Summary of Events and Information	Remarks and references to Appendices
CORDONNERIE BOUTILLERIE SECTOR	JULY 28	4:-	B gun will give short bursts of covering fire from Zero hour until the raiding parties are established in their posts in the enemy line. The Officer in charge of this gun will be in communication with the O.C. raid, and will continue short bursts until ordered by the O.C. raid to do so to cease fire. The remaining guns i.e. C, X and Y, will not fire at all until the Artillery [guns] on which they are all guns will depend fire and "antiaircraft" same for 5 minutes when they will gradually give off, taking their cue from the artillery.	
"	29		Situation normal. 2000 rounds fired by No 2 gun in accordance with Brigade Operation Order 52 (repeated with a few amendments) (for particulars of Barrel operation order 52, see July 27). 12 rounds fired at aircraft.	
"	30		Situation normal. 3000 rounds fired in accordance with Brigade Operation Order No 60 on FME DE LA MARLAQUE N.17.b.30.73. and NEBULA'S WITCH at N.12.b.35.21.	

Army Form C. 2118.

WAR DIARY
or
INTELLIGENCE SUMMARY.
(Erase heading not required.)

Place	Date	Hour	Summary of Events and Information	Remarks and references to Appendices
CORDONNERIE BOUTILLERIE SECTOR	July 1		Situation normal. 1000 rounds fired on O.14.40.75 & O.1.a.13.68.	

WAR DIARY of 170 MACHINE GUN COY

Army Form C. 2118.

INTELLIGENCE SUMMARY. — For AUGUST 1916

Vol 7

Place	Date	Hour	Summary of Events and Information	Remarks and references to Appendices
CORDONNERIE -BOUTILLERIE SECTOR	1ST		Situation normal. Wire received from Division that Capt H.B. Law appointed 2/C No 9 O/o 20th Division with rank of Major. Lieut. Barraclough appointed O/C Company with acting rank of Captain.	
"	2ND		Situation normal. 1000 rounds fired from H.34.b.25.38 at NEBULA SWITCH N.12 t.05.54 to N.12 t.36.42.	
"	"		Arrangements completed for Relief of 141 M.G. Coy in the ARMENTIERES SECTOR.	
"	3rd	11.A.M.	No. 2 Section - BOUTILLERIE SUB-SECTOR relieved by No 3 Section of 171 M.G. Cy.	
"	"	11.30pm	No. 1 Section proceeded by Motor Lorry to relieve Section of 171 M.G Coy holding SUBSIDIARY LINE in HOUPLINES SECTOR.	
"	"		1000 rounds fired from H.34.b.25.38 at CHATEAU RICHE ROAD N.11.d.45.48.	
"	4th	5.0AM	Section of 141 M.G. Cy relieved by No. 1 Section 170 M.G Cy arrived at MARTYN LODGE.	
"	"	2.PM	No. 3 Section 170 M.G. Coy (Right Section) relieved by this Section.	
"	"	4.30 PM	No. 2 Section, 170 M.G Coy proceeded by Motor Lorry to relieve Section of 141 M.G. Coy holding Centre Section of ARMENTIERES SECTOR.	
"	"		1000 rounds fired from H.34.b.25.33 at NEBULA SWITCH N.12.b.0.7.45 to N.12.t.30.18.	
"	5TH	1.0AM	Major Law proceeded to join his Division.	
"	"		Section of 141 M.G Coy relieved by No.2 Section arrived at MARTYN LODGE.	
"	"	12.30.PM	HEADQUARTERS AND TRANSPORT moved. Headquarters to C.25.c.25.405.	
"	"		Transferred to H.13.d.80.80.	
"	"	11.0am	No. 4 Section. 170 M.G. Coy relieved by Section of 141 M.G. Coy.	

Army Form C. 2118.

WAR DIARY
or
INTELLIGENCE SUMMARY.

(Erase heading not required.)

Instructions regarding War Diaries and Intelligence Summaries are contained in F. S. Regs., Part II. and the Staff Manual respectively. Title pages will be prepared in manuscript.

Place	Date	Hour	Summary of Events and Information	Remarks and references to Appendices
ARMENTIERES SECTOR	5TH	7.30 PM	No. 3 Section 141 M.G.Coy proceeded by Motor Lorry to relieve section of 141. M.G.Coy holding L'EPINETTE Sector. 1,250 rounds fired at HOUSE @ 20.V. 35.50 and in answer to S.O.S. signal.	
"	6TH	"	Section of 141. M.G.Coy relieved by No. 3 Section 170 M.G.Coy, arrived at MARTIN LODGE at 11.0.AM.	
"	"	2.30 PM	No. 4 Section 141. M.G.Coy proceeded by Motor Lorry to relieve Section of 173 M.G.Coy holding SUPPORT LINE in HOUPLINES SECTOR. (19R. Pte Douglas, wounded by shrapnel. New defence scheme in course of construction.	
"	7TH	"	Situation normal. 3,500 rounds fired from (1) I.4.a.33.80 at ROAD. I.18.Q.35.75 (2) I.14.7.20.00. (2) I.9.T.10.10 at WEZ MACQUART. (3) Left Sector on ROAD @ 30.a.80.05.16 @ 30.d.35.30	
"	8TH	"	Situation normal. 1,000 rounds fired from @ 8.C. 40.90, on HOUSE and ROAD C.18.d.20.10 do 1,000 rounds fired from C.28.c. at FME du CHASTEL and ROAD at C.18.d.20.10	
"	9TH	"	650 rounds fired from I.9.T.30.40. at INNER AVENUE. 650 rounds fired from I.9.T.10.10 at FME RUE DE LA BLANCHE	
"	10TH	"	Situation normal. 1.9R. Killed (Pte HARRISON F) 1.9R Shell shock. 650 rounds fired from I.3.a.60.10 at I.18.a.25.45. 650 rounds fired from C.28.c at TEMPLE ROAD from I.4.a.53.80 at C.30.d.87.00. 1,000 rounds fired from C.28.c at TEMPLE ROAD at C.30.d.90.00.	
"	11TH	"	Situation normal. 450 rounds fired from C.26.c.2. at C.18.d.2.1. FME du CHASTEL 850 rounds fired from I.3.d.6.2. at CROSS ROADS I.18.a. 850 rounds fired from I.9.T.I.I. at INCARNATE AVENUE. 950 rounds fired from I.H.d.53.80 at C.3.d.87.00.	

WAR DIARY or INTELLIGENCE SUMMARY

Army Form C. 2118.

Place	Date	Hour	Summary of Events and Information	Remarks and references to Appendices
ARMENTIERES SECTOR	12TH		Situation normal. 1,000 rounds fired from C.29.c.1 at ROAD @ 30.T.8.8.& C.30.T.98.86	
"	"		750 rounds from I.3.d.6.2 at INCARNATE COMMUNICATOR I.17.?	
"	"		450 rounds from I.H.a.53.80. at JUNCTION of TRAMS C.3.7.15.23.	
"	13TH		Situation normal. 500 rounds from I.9.T.3.4. at INANE AVENUE. 500 rounds from I.9.T.1.1. at FME RUE DE LA BLANCHE. 500 rounds from I.3.d.6.3 at INCENSE COMM-UNICATOR. I.17.a. 500 rounds from I.H.a.53.80. at INANE ALLEY. I.5.d.4.6 to I.12.a.1.3. 10-00 rounds from C.28.c.1 at JUNCTION of ROAD and TRENCH at C.30.d.45.64.	
"	14TH		Situation normal. 500 rounds from I.3.d.6.2 at INANE DRIVE I.12.a. 500 rounds from I.H.a.53.80. at ROAD and INANE ALLEY I.18.a.25.43 to I.17.?.2.6. 500 rounds from I.9.T.1.1. at INCIDENT DRIVE AND ALLEY. 500 rounds from I.9.3.5.4 at INANE AVENUE. 450 rounds from C.28.c.2 at FME DU CHASTEL C.18.d.2.1	
"	15TH		Situation normal. 450 rounds from C.28.c.3 at FME DU CHASTEL C.18.d.2.1. 500 rounds from I.3.A.6.2 at INCENCE COMMUNICATOR I.17.a. 500 rounds from I.H.a.53.80. at 1.18.a.25.43 to I.17.?.20.00. 500 rounds from I.9.?.6.10. at FME DE LA BLANCHE. 500 rounds from I.9.2.3.4. at INANE AVENUE.	
"	16TH		Situation normal. 500 rounds from I.9.T.3.4 at JUNCTION of INCARNATE and INCENSE AVENUE. 1,000 rounds from C.28.c.1. at ROAD C.30.T.8.8.16 @.30.T.98.86	
"	17TH		Situation normal. 500 rounds from I.9.T.1.1. at FME RUELLE ME 19 BLANCHE. 500 rounds from I.9.T.3.4 at INANE AVENUE and HOUSE. 450 rounds from C.28.c.1 at JUNCTION of ROAD and TRENCH C.30.d.45.64.	
"	"		L'EPINETTE SECTOR. New "MACHINE GUN SCHEME FOR DEFENCE OF THE HOUPLINES AND L'EPINETTE SECTORS" came into operation on this sector on this day.	
"	"		"Number of Machine Guns in the Salient & Subsidiary Line 12. Number of Machine Guns in Reserve 4	

Army Form C. 2118.

WAR DIARY
or
INTELLIGENCE SUMMARY
(Erase heading not required.)

Place	Date	Hour	Summary of Events and Information	Remarks and references to Appendices
ARMENTIERES SECTOR	17TH		FRONT LINE SYSTEM.	
			1. The present scheme of holding the front line by night consists of 14 Infantry posts situated in the Front Line, supported by 5 Machine Guns and 20 Lewis Guns situated in or near the Support Line. These guns cover the stretches of the front line between the Infantry posts.	
			2. In order to give a margin of safety to the Infantry in the front line posts, stakes are erected 30 yards on the right and left flanks of the posts. The Machine Guns and Lewis Guns are laid on these stakes it defines extent of traverse is thus allotted to each gun.	
			3. The guns are "stopped" by means of angle irons etc. driven in the ground making it impossible to traverse beyond the correct limits. The guns are laid to fire into the front line parapet, and registration tests are carried out occasionally where necessary by arrangement with the Infantry.	
			4. In the event of one of the Infantry posts being attacked by the enemy, the post in question will send up a Green Very Light, on which cool the Machine Guns and Lewis Guns on its immediate flanks will open fire. If the post requires fulfilled support in addition to Machine Gun support, a Red "Very" light will be sent up, on which case the Machine Guns and Lewis Guns on its immediate flank will open fire as in the case of a Green "Very Light".	
			5. In case of foggy or misty weather the same dispositions of Infantry posts and Machine Guns will be adopted as at night. The Infantry will	

WAR DIARY or INTELLIGENCE SUMMARY

Place	Date	Hour	Summary of Events and Information	Remarks and references to Appendices
ARMENTIERES	17/12		warn the Officers Commanding the Machine Gun Sections in the line as soon as they intend to occupy the front line Posts.	
"			b Machine Gun Section Officers and Infantry Company Commanders are responsible for seeing that all Machine Guns and Lewis Guns in their Sectors are correctly "Stopped", so as to be clear of the Posts, and for seeing that their men thoroughly understand the precautions to be taken to prevent firing into our Posts.	
"			Y Infantry Company Commanders are responsible for seeing that a stiff board is always in position 30 yards clear of the flank bay of each Post, to enable the Machine Gun and Lewis Gun teams to adjust their "stopping" sights daily. The board on the right of each Post will have a diagonal black cross on it. The board on the left will have a red circle on it.	
"			6/ Section Officers will carry out frequent tests of the elevation of Machine Guns and Lewis Guns by arrangement with Infantry Company Commanders.	
"			9 Definite hours, between which "Stopping" Machine Gun and Lewis Gun fire are to be employed, will be notified weekly to O.C. Machine Gun Company. Section Officers are responsible that no "stopping" fire is employed except between these hours. The greatest care must be taken to make all ranks of the Machine Gun and Lewis Gun Sections thoroughly understand that they only use "stopping" fire between these hours, and at no other times.	
"			Section Officers will warn all their N.C.O.s and men that they run the risk of being shot by our own fire if they are in the intervals between the night posts during the hours laid down for "stopping" Machine Gun and Lewis Gun fire. That accidents due to "stopping fire will in 9.9 cases out of 100, be due to carelessness in seeing that all hands know their orders.	

WAR DIARY or INTELLIGENCE SUMMARY

Army Form C. 2118.

Place	Date	Hour	Summary of Events and Information	Remarks and references to Appendices
ARMENTIERES SECTOR	17TH		10. Patrols. Careful arrangements must be made for the exit and return of all patrols, owing to the wide gaps between the Posts. Reconnoitring patrols will not cause so much noise at the Machine Gun and Lewis Gun "stopping" fire but arrangements will be made for battle patrols, most careful steps being taken to define clearly their sphere of action.	
			11. "Very" lights. At least 24 "Very" lights will be kept at each Machine Gun emplacement, in the support line and subsidiary line, and No. 6 Os in charge of teams will be responsible for keeping their "Very" lights dry.	
			12. Every Machine Gun and Lewis Gun, where possible, must have an alternate position from which the same ground can be covered as from the original position.	
			13. In accordance with para. 3 of Brigade Instructions No. 16, Section Officers Commanding guns in each Battalion Sector will report daily to the Battalion Commanders in their own Sector. During periods of S.O.S. or enemy attack, the Section Officers whose Headquarters are at SQUARE FARM, will be either at Right Battalion Headquarters or at some signal station from which he will be in direct telephonic communication with the Right Battalion Commander.	
			14. The Senior Section Officers at SQUARE FARM and TISSAGE will visit the LEWIS Gun positions in the Right and Left Battalion Sectors respectively twice, or at least once a week. They will generally supervise the Lewis guns as regards mountings, elevations, directions, etc.	

WAR DIARY or INTELLIGENCE SUMMARY

Army Form C. 2118.

Place	Date	Hour	Summary of Events and Information	Remarks and references to Appendices
ARMENTIERES SECTOR	17TH		SUBSIDIARY LINE	
"	"		1. The defence of the Subsidiary Line consists of a belt of Machine Gun fire established by Machine Guns and Lewis Guns.	
"	"		2. Under normal circumstances this belt of fire will be established by 7 Machine Guns and 4 Lewis Guns.	
"	"		3. One section of the Machine Gun Company will be kept at Company Head-Quarters, momentarily, as constituting a mobile reserve, which will be at the disposal of the G.O.C. Brigade.	
"	"		4. In the event of the Subsidiary Line having to be defended the 4 Machine Guns in Reserve will be moved up into the Subsidiary Line, and take over the positions normally held by Lewis Guns. Until the Machine Guns arrive the Lewis Guns will do their part in establishing a belt of fire. Ha. Machine Gun trench mountings with Lewis Gun adaptors will be erected at each of these 4 positions.	
"	18TH		Situation normal. 850 rounds fired from I.9.2.3.4 at FME RUEUE DE LA BAROCHE. 850 rounds fired from I.3.d.6.2 at CROSS ROADS I.18.a. 850 rounds from I.a.a. 53.80 at INCARNATE AVENUE. 450 rounds from C.26.c.1 at TRAMWAYS C.30.b.90.45 500 rounds from C.28.c.2 at C.18.d.2.1.	
"	19TH		450 rounds fired from C.28.c.2 at TEMPLE and ROAD at C.30.d.90.60. 500 rounds fired from I.9.6.10.10. at INCIDENT DRIVE and ALLEY. Situation normal. 450 rounds from C.28.c.l at ROAD at C.30.b.80.60	
"	20TH		@ 30.b.98.66. 950 rounds from C.28.c.2 at FME DE CHAPEL C.19.d.20.10. 500 rounds I.9.2.30.40. at INANE AVENUE. 500 rounds from I.a.a.53.80 at TRAM JUNCTION at C.30.7.15.23. 2/Lt G.H. Grace arrived from 213 M.G.Coy to assume duties of Second-in-Command	

WAR DIARY
or
INTELLIGENCE SUMMARY

Army Form C. 2118.

Place	Date	Hour	Summary of Events and Information	Remarks and references to Appendices
ARMENTIERES SECTOR	21ST		Company Headquarters moved to H.6.b.7.12.9½. Situation normal. 500 rounds from No.1. position at JUNCTION OF TRENCH and ROAD at C.30.d.87.10. 500 rounds from No.3 at INCARNATE C.T. 500 rounds from No.1. at INANE AVENUE and NOOSE. BRIGADE O.O. No 65 received for night 21st + 22nd. Machine Guns to cover area C.11.c.80.80 to C.17.a.90.40. C.17.d.70.00 to C.17.a.30.00 by means of indirect fire. From Zero minus 30 to Zero, short intermittent bursts will be fired. After Zero the duration of these bursts will be doubled and slowed in S.O.S. signal go up fire will be increased to the maximum intensity.	
"	22ND		Situation normal. O.O. No 65 cancelled. Wind was unfavourable. 500 rounds fired from I.9.b.10.10. at I.17.b.30.60. 500 rounds from I.9.7.30.70 at INANE AVENUE and HOUSE. 500 rounds fired from I.3.d.65.50 at I.5.d.45.05. 450 rounds from C.28.C.2 at C.18.d.20.10.	
"	23RD		Situation normal. O.O. No.65 cancelled. Wind unfavourable. 500 rounds from I.3.d.60.30. at I.8.a.63.98 CROSS ROADS. 500 rounds from I.9.7.10.10. at FME RUELLE DE LA BLANCHE. 1000 fired at Aeroplane. 3,500 fired in conjunction with O.O. 65 as Wire cancelling O.O. was delayed.	
"	24TH		Situation normal. Brigade O.O. 65 carried out. 3,500 rounds fired in connection with same. 600 rounds fired from I.3.d.60.20 at I.18.a.65.98. 600 rounds from I.a. 53.80 at I.18.a.25. I.5.16 I.17.b.20.00. 600 rounds fired from I.9.7.30.40 at INCARNATE and INCENSE AVENUES.	
"	25TH		Situation normal. 450 rounds fired from I.9.7.10.10 at WEZ MACQUET. 450 rounds from I.3.d.65.30 at I.17.a.37.50. 450 rounds from I.4.a.53.80 at I.5.d.90.10. 1000 rounds from C.28.C.-1 at C.30.b.80.80 to C.30.7.98.86. 800 rounds fired at Aeroplanes.	
"	26TH		Situation normal. Company Headquarters shelled from 7.30 to 9.30.a.m. Company Headquarters moved to B.30.C.30.10. New scheme of Defence for Frontlines Sector introduced (see Aug 17th) 2,000 rounds fired on Aeroplanes. 1,000 rounds fired from C.28.C.2 at C.32.d.90.00. 500 rounds from I.9.7.10.10 on FME RUELLE DE LA BLANCHE.	

Army Form C. 2118.

WAR DIARY
or
INTELLIGENCE SUMMARY.
(Erase heading not required.)

Place	Date	Hour	Summary of Events and Information	Remarks and references to Appendices
ARMENTIERES SECTOR	27TH		Situation normal. No 3 Section in rest at Headquarters. 500 rounds fired from I.9.b.30.70 at INANE AVENUE. 750 rounds from C.28.c.2 at C.18.d.20.10. 750 rounds from C.22.c.1 at C.18.a.90.40 to C.18.d.20.95.	
"	28TH		Situation normal. 750 rounds fired from I.9.b.10.10 at I.23.a.05.70 to I.23.a.35.35. 1000 rounds fired from C.22.c.1 at C.18.a.90.40 to C.18.a.20.95.	
"	29TH		Situation normal. 750 rounds fired from C.28.c-1 at C.30.d.30.62.b. C.30.d.45.64. 750 rounds from C.28.c.2 at C.30.a.90.00. 650 rounds from I.9.b.10.10 at I.23.a.14.24.b. I.23.c.45.95. 650 rounds from I.9.b.30.70 at I.18.a.80.95.b. I.12.b.05.70. 50 rounds Registration	
"	30TH		Situation normal. 1000 rounds fired from C.28.c-1 at R2R2 C.30.b.80.80. C.30.b.98.36. 1000 rounds from C.3.b.c.2 at F75 DU CHASTEL at C.19.d.28. 500 rounds fired from I.9.b.10.10 at WEZ MACQUART I.23.a.35.35. 500 rounds fired from I.9.b.30.70 at INANE AVENUE I.12.a.50.95.b. I.6.d.40.20.	
"	31st		Situation normal. 750 rounds fired from C.38.c.2 at C.30.d.90.00 to I.6.b.00.70. 750 rounds from C.22.c-1 at C.17.d.20.95. 1750 rounds from I.9.b.10.10 at I.17.b.d. I.23.a.35.35. 1000 fired at Aeroplanes.	
"	24TH		A machine gun barrage has been arranged to be put down on the enemy communication trenches and support lines by our guns in the subsidiary line in case of S.O.S.	

To Headquarters,
   57th Division

3/10/17

Herewith War Diary of the
170th Machine Gun Company
for the month of September
1917.

DVBarron 2nd Lt
for O.C. 170 M.G. Coy.

Orderly Room stamp: Reference No. 135, 170 M.G. Coy

WAR DIARY
or
INTELLIGENCE SUMMARY

Army Form C. 2118.

of 170 Machine Gun Company

In the Field. September 1917

Place	Date	Hour	Summary of Events and Information	Remarks and references to Appendices
ARMENTIERES	1st		Situation normal. 5750 rounds fired from :- (1) I.9.b.30.70. (2) I.9.b.10.10 on I.5.b.6. (3) C.28-1 on C.30.b.70.75. (4) C.28-2 on C.18.d.20.20 to C.18.d.25.50. (5) Fired on Aeroplane. 1600 rounds. Registration. 250 rounds.	
"	2nd		Situation normal. 3000 rounds fired from (1) I.9.b.10.10 on I.23.a.12.27. (2) I.23.c.45.95. (2) I.9.b.30.70 on I.12.a.20.80. (3) I.23.a.50.28. (3) C.28.2 on C.30.d.08.76 to C.30.d.35.74. (4) C.38.1 on C.18.c.20.20 to C.18.d.10.40.	
"	3rd		Situation normal. No. 3 Section relieved No. 4 Section in Machine Gun Section No. 4 Section coming to Company Headquarters. 3000 rounds fired from :- (1) I.9.b-16.10 on I.17.b.30.10 (2) I.9.b.30.70 on I.11.b.05.10 to I.11.d.85.85. (3) C.28-1 on C.30.b.80.80 to C.30.d.88.96. (4) C.23-1 on C.18.c.80.80 to C.18.d.10.40. (5) 250 rounds fired on aircraft.	
"	4/5		Situation normal. No. 1 Section relieved No. 2 Section who were moved to Subsidiary positions vacated by No. 1 Section. 750 rounds fired from I.9.1 on I.23.a. 17.27 to I.23.c.45.95. 7.30 " I.9.2 on I.12.a.50.95. I.6 d.40.10.	
"	5th		Situation normal. 1000 rounds fired from I.9.1 on ROAD JUNCTION at I.17.b.30.10. 1000 rounds fired from I.9.2 on INANE AVENUE I.12.a.20.80 to I.12.a.50.80. 500 rounds fired from C.28.c.40.90 at FRIZ du CHASTEL @ 18.d.20.10. 500 rounds from C.28.c.6.5.20 at TRAMWAYS at C.30.3.70.75.	
"	6th		Situation normal. 500 rounds fired at Aircraft. 500 rounds fired from I.9.1 at I.23.a.17.27 to I.6.b.10.10. 200 rounds fired from I.9.2 at I.23.a.17.27 to I.23.a.17.95. 250 rounds from O.22.c.40.65 at I.C.18.d.60.58.	

WAR DIARY
—or—
INTELLIGENCE SUMMARY
(Erase heading not required.)

Army Form C. 2118.

Place	Date	Hour	Summary of Events and Information	Remarks and references to Appendices
ARMENTIERES	7TH		Situation normal. 1,000 rounds fired from I.9.1. at I.23.a.05.70.10. I.23.a.35.35. 1,000 rounds fired from I.9.2. at I.12.a.20.80 to I.12.a.50.80. 750 rounds fired from I.3.d.60.20. at I.11.a.90.18.16. I.17.b.35.20.	
"	8TH		Situation normal. 500 rounds fired at Aircraft. 500 rounds from I.9.1. at I.23.a.05.70.63. 28.c.90.90. on I.6.a.60.05. 500 rounds fired from C.27.c.40.63. at C./8.d.20.10. 1000 rounds fired from I.9.1. at I.23.a.17.27.60. I.23.a.45.95. 1000 rounds fired from I.9.2. at I.18.a.65.95. I.18.a.95.10.	
"	9TH		Situation normal. 950 rounds fired from I.3.a.60.20. at I.11.d.90.05. 1,000 rounds fired from I.9.1. at I.18.a.55.80.16 I.17.b.30.10. 1000 rounds fired from I.9.2. at I.18.a.80.95.16 I.12.b.05.20.	
"	10TH		Situation normal. No.4 Section relieved No.2 Section who came to Company Headquarters. 1,000 rounds fired from I.9.1. at I.17.c.45.55.15. I.17.c.69.40. 1,000 rounds fired from I.9.2. at I.18.a.65.98. 250 rounds fired from C.22.1. at C.18.a.90.49.	
"	11TH		Situation normal. 500 rounds fired on aircraft. 750 rounds fired from C.28.2. at D.19.c.12.50.16 D.19.c.50.60. 750 rounds fired from C.28.1. at C.30.7.21.32.16 D.25.a.34.56. 1,000 rounds fired from I.9.1. at I.23.a.19.24.16 I.23.c.45.95. 1,000 rounds fired from I.9.2. at I.12.a.40.95.16 I.6.d.40.60.	
"	12TH		Situation normal. 1,000 rounds fired from I.9.1. at I.23.a.17.29.16 I.23.c.45.95. 1000 rounds from I.9.2. at I.18.a.60.95. 750 rounds fired from C.30.c.22.45. 450 rounds fired from C.28.c. 15.60 at C.30.c.48.66.	
"	13TH		Situation normal. 750 rounds fired from C.22.1. at C.D.6.d.24.18.	

WAR DIARY
or
INTELLIGENCE SUMMARY

Army Form C. 2118.

Place	Date	Hour	Summary of Events and Information	Remarks and references to Appendices
ARMENTIERES	13th		750 rounds fired from C.38.2 at D.25.a.12.59 and D.25.c.65.34.	
"	"		1,000 rounds fired from I.9.1. at I.17.6.30.10. 1,000 rounds fired from I.9.2. at I.18.a.80.95-b I.12.b.05.20.	
"	14th		Retaliation normal. 750 rounds fired from C.38.c.65.20 at C.36.d.10.64. 1000 rounds fired from I.9.1. at I.19. c.45.55-b I.14 c.19.40. 1000 rounds fired from I.9.2. at I.18.a.65.98 1000 rounds fired from I.3. at F.8.d.68.34.	
"	"		Advance party of 115 Machine Gun Company arrived.	
"	15th		Retaliation normal. 115 M.G.C. arrived at Company Head quarters at 9.30 p.m. The sections in the line were relieved during the night Sept. 15th/16th. Relief completed by 5.30 a.m. Following are the Relief Orders for the Relief at 140 M.G.C. by the 115 M.G.Co. on the night of the 15th/16th September, 1917:-	
"	"		No. 1 Section of 115 M.G. Coy will relieve No. 1 Section 140 M.G Coy	
"	"		" 2 " " " " " " 2 " "	
"	"		" 3 " " " " " " 3 " "	
"	"		" 4 " " " " " " 4 " "	
"	"		The exact times of the relief cannot be stated. It is anticipated that the 115 M.G.Coy with their Transport complete will arrive at these Headquarters about 10 p.m. 15/9/17.	
"	"		GUIDES. Officers Commanding Sections will have one guide per Section at Company Headquarters at 8 p.m. on 15th.	

WAR DIARY
INTELLIGENCE SUMMARY
(Erase heading not required.)

Army Form C. 2118.

Place	Date	Hour	Summary of Events and Information	Remarks and references to Appendices
ARMENTIERES	15/4		This guide must be an N.C.O. They will also arrange for one guide per team to be at Section Headquarters not later than 9 P.M on 15th.	
"	"		LIMBERS. The Transport Officer will arrange for 2 limbers to be at TISSAGE at 11.P.M on 15TH (i.e one limber for No 3 Section and one limber for No 4 Section). He will also arrange for one limber to be at SQUARE FARM at 11.P.M on 15TH for No 1 Section	
"	"		On the arrival of the various sections of the relieving company at the respective Section Headquarters, guides will conduct teams to their emplacements. Section Sergeants will report when the relief is complete to Section Officer. Section Officer will hand over all maps, log books, trench stores etc to the relieving Officer and obtain receipts in duplicate, as previously indicated. Gun teams will load their guns, tripods, etc on the limbers and Sections will then proceed to Company Headquarters where they will stay for the remainder of the night.	
"	"		RATIONS. No rations will be sent up the line on the night of 15th. C.Q.M.S will make arrangements for hot beans of tea to be kept in readiness from 12 midnight until the last Section has arrived at Company Headquarters. The Headquarters and Store of the relieving	

WAR DIARY
INTELLIGENCE SUMMARY

(Erase heading not required.)

Army Form C. 2118.

Place	Date	Hour	Summary of Events and Information	Remarks and references to Appendices
ARMENTIERES	15th		Company will be in the billet opposite the 170th Company Orderly Room, for the night of 15/16th and will remain there until the Headquarters of the 170th Company are vacated.	
"	"		BELT BOXES. 1st Belt boxes per gun on the line will be handed over to the relieving Company. The relieving Company will dump their belt boxes at Company Headquarters on their way up the line, and they will be automatically taken over by sections of 170 Company on their arrival at Company Headquarters.	
"	"		ANTI-AIRCRAFT SIGHTS. Anti-aircraft sights are not kept fitted and will be taken with the Company.	
"	"		TRENCH STANDING ORDERS. The copies of French Standing orders will also be taken with the Company.	
"	"		Section Officers will report completion of relief on arrival at Company Headquarters.	
"	"		The Company will move by section to JESUS FARM CAMP at B.20 a 1.8 on 16/8/17. The first section will leave Company Headquarters at 10 a.m. and will proceed to this camp via Erquinghem Bridge.	
"	"		No. 2 Section. The Transport Officer will arrange for the three limbers of No. 2 section to be at Company Headquarters	

WAR DIARY
or
INTELLIGENCE SUMMARY

(Erase heading not required.)

Army Form C. 2118.

Place	Date	Hour	Summary of Events and Information	Remarks and references to Appendices
ARMENTIERES	15TH		at 5 P.M on 15TH. These limbers will then proceed to the Transport lines at JESUS FARM CAMP. B.20.a.1.8. No.2 Section will be the first Section to move from Company Headquarters and will leave at 10.a.m. 16/9/17. Dress - full marching order, with Steel helmets carried on packs, water bottles filled. Service caps will be worn.	
"	"		No.3. SECTION. The Transport Officer will arrange for the 3. limbers of No.3 Section to be at Company Headquarters at 9.30. a.m. on 16TH. O.C. No.3. Section will then load his limbers and proceed to JESUS FARM CAMP leaving Company Headquarters at 10.30.a.m. Dress etc, as for No.2 Section.	
"	"		No.4. SECTION. The Transport Officer will arrange for the three limbers of No.4. Section to be at Company Headquarters at 10.30.a.m. on 16TH. O.C. No.4 Section will load his limbers and proceed to JESUS FARM CAMP, leaving Company Headquarters at 11.30. AM. Dress etc, as for No.2. Section	
"	"		No.1 SECTION. The Transport Officer will arrange for the three limbers of No.1. Section to be at Company Headquarters at 11.30.a.m. on 16TH. O.C. No.1 Section will then load his limbers and proceed to JESUS FARM CAMP, leaving Company Headquarters at 12.30. P.M.	
"	"		HEADQUARTERS. The Transport Officer will arrange for the Head-	

WAR DIARY or INTELLIGENCE SUMMARY

Army Form C. 2118.

Place	Date	Hour	Summary of Events and Information	Remarks and references to Appendices
ARMENTIERES	15TH		quarters, limbers to be at Company Headquarters at 10 a.m. on	
"	16/9/17		The Company Cook, under the orders of C.Q.M.S., will put all his tackle on Headquarters limber and proceed at once to JESUS FARM CAMP. Headquarters limbers will then return to Company Headquarters for the purpose of moving Orderly Room, Cobblers and Officers tackle etc etc, and will then proceed to JESUS FARM CAMP under Corporal Cart.	
"	"		OFFICERS KIT. Officers Kit will be carried on their own Section limbers for the purpose of the move. The Transport Officer is attached to No. 3 Section and his kit will go on No. 3 Section limber.	
"	"		TRANSPORT. The Transport Section will move to JESUS FARM CAMP and will take over the lines there by 4 P.M. 15/9/17. The Transport Officer will arrange for Sgt. Megannan to be at our old Transport lines at 11 P.M. on 15TH and wait there until the Transport of the relieving Company arrive, which will be sometime before dawn on 16/9/17.	
"	"		2ND Lt. Ballantine will proceed to JESUS FARM CAMP to take over the Camp, to be there at 10 a.m. 15/9/17. He will take with him his Kit and rations. The Transport Officer will arrange for the Mess Cart to be at Company Headquarters at 8 a.m. 15/9/17 for the purpose of carrying Mr Ballantines Kit.	

WAR DIARY or INTELLIGENCE SUMMARY

Army Form C. 2118.

Place	Date	Hour	Summary of Events and Information	Remarks and references to Appendices
ARMENTIERES TO JESUS FARM CAMP B.20.a.20.80.	16TH		Sections proceeded independently to JESUS FARM CAMP, the last section No 1, arriving at 2.30.p.m.	
"	17TH		Cleaning and parking of Gun and Limber Kit.	
"	18TH		" " " " " " " " " "	
From B.20.a.20.80 to LA GORGUE L.28.c.20.70	19TH		Company marched with Brigade, having starting point R.8#9 Junction G.b.d.20.60 at 10.51 a.m. thence by CROIX DU BAC – ESTAIRES, road N of River LYS – CROSS ROADS, L.29.7.00.60 to billets at L.28 C 20.70.	
To BUSNES at P.31.c.60.40	19TH		Brigade march continued, having starting point at 8.4 a.m. at Road Junction K.35.b.30.30. thence by LE GRAND PACAUT – CALONNE SUR-LA-LYS – ROBECQ – BRIDGE, P.27.b.30.50 to billets in BUSNES at P.31.C.60.40.	
To LA TIRMANDE S.6.a.25.30	20TH		Brigade march continued, having starting point – U.R.d 50.85 at 9.13 a.m. thence through ECQUEDECQUES – FAUQUENHEM – AUCHY-AU-BOIS – LA TIRMANDE S.6.a.25.30.	
"	21ST		Cleaning of Gun Kit and Limber Kit.	
"	22ND		Cleaning of Gun Kit and Limber Kit.	
"	23RD		Billet and Kit Inspection. 1 section moved to S.3.a.50.90. owing to shortage of water.	
"	24TH		Company Training.	
"	25TH		Company Training.	
"	26TH		Company Training.	

Army Form C. 2118.

WAR DIARY
~~INTELLIGENCE SUMMARY~~
(Erase heading not required.)

Instructions regarding War Diaries and Intelligence Summaries are contained in F. S. Regs., Part II. and the Staff Manual respectively. Title Pages will be prepared in manuscript.

Place	Date	Hour	Summary of Events and Information	Remarks and references to Appendices
LA TUREMANDE	27th		Company Training - Route March	
"	28th		do. do.	
"	29th		do. do.	
"	30th		do. do.	

M. Mackman Lieut
2nd
O.C. 170 M.G. Coy.

WAR DIARY OF THE 170TH MACHINE GUN COMPANY
INTELLIGENCE SUMMARY
IN THE FIELD

Army Form C. 2118.

Place	Date	Hour	Summary of Events and Information	Remarks and references to Appendices
LA TIREMANDE	Oct. 1st		Company training. 32 Infantry reported. 3 form each Battalion of Brigade. 2/5 K.O.Y.L.I. Regt. attached to No.1 Section, 2/4th K.O.Y.L.I. Regt. to No.2 Section, 2/5 Y.L. Regt. attached to No.3 Section, 4/5 Y.L. Regt. to No.4 Section.	
"	2nd		Company training.	
"	3rd		Company training.	
"	4th		Company route march, via LIGNY-LEZ-AIRE, WESTREHEM, FONTAINE-LEZ-HERMANS, AUCHY-AU-BOIS.	
"	5th		Company training.	
"	6th		Brigade inspection by F.M. Sir Douglas Haig.	
"	7th		Field day with Brigade in Brigade Training Area at ENGUINEGATTE. No.1 Section attached to Infantry and advanced to objective. Nos. 2, 3 and 4 Sections formed a practice barrage.	
"	8th		Company training.	
"	9th		Company training. Brigade Field day washed out owing to excessive rain.	
"	10th		Company training.	
"	11th		Barrage at ENGUINEGATTE carried out by 8 guns from each of 170, 171, 172, 173 Companies. 16000 rounds (approx.) fired by our guns.	
"	12th		Brigade field day in training area at ENGUINEGATTE. One Section attached to each Battalion.	
"	13th		Company training. Inspection by O.C. Coy. Preparations for move.	
"	14th		Move postponed. Company training.	
"	15th		Company training.	

WAR DIARY of the 170TH MACHINE GUN COMPANY
INTELLIGENCE SUMMARY
IN THE FIELD

Army Form C. 2118.

Place	Date	Hour	Summary of Events and Information	Remarks and references to Appendices
LA-TRENANDE	Oct. 16		Company training and preparations for move.	
"	" 17		Company marched with Brigade to RENESCURE (near ST. OMER) passing starting point RAILWAY BRIDGE at ESTREE BLANCHE at 11.27am, via BASSE BOULOGNE CROSS ROADS, MARTHES, MAMETZ, ROQUETOIRE, QUIESTEDE and BELLE CROIX.	
RENESCURE	" 18		Company proceeded by motor lorries to PROVEN, via HAZEBROUCK, STEENVOORDE and WATOU, to PLAISTOWE CAMP, No. 2 Billeting Area, PROVEN. Transport by road.	
PROVEN	" 19		In camp, cleaning and inspection of equipment.	
"	" 20		PLAISTOWE CAMP.	
"	" 21		PLAISTOWE CAMP. Church parade.	
"	" 22		PLAISTOWE CAMP. Officer sent forward to MARSOUIN FARM, 28 C.8.4.60.20.	
"	" 23		Company proceeded by train from PROVEN to BOESINGHE, hence by road to MARSOUIN FARM CAMP. 25% Officers and O/R excluding Transport and attached Infantry sent to Corps Reinforcement Camp at HERZEELE, on Transport Lines. Transport proceeded by road to MALAKOFF AREA. Company bivouaced at MARSOUIN FARM.	
ALKEMRIDGE	" 24		Coys. Bivouaough proceeded to Company Headquarters at LOUIS FARM U.2.H.a.5.0.10. At 4.0pm Transport brought guns and equipment of Nos. 1 and 2 sections to Road at C. & Central Entrance they were manhandled to LOUIS FARM, each team carrying gun, tripod, spare parts case, 6 belt boxes and 16 strips of belt containing 50 rounds each in trundlers, as well as four days hard rations. One was to LOUIS FARM, and team	

Army Form C. 2118.

WAR DIARY
or
INTELLIGENCE SUMMARY
(Erase heading not required.)

Place	Date	Hour	Summary of Events and Information	Remarks and references to Appendices
AUBERS RIDGE	Oct 1st		No. 2 Section was practically out, together with several men of No. 1 Section. The remaining guns, together with several men of No. 1 Section, proceeded to LOUIS FARM. No.1 Section remained in EAGLE TRENCH for the night, while No. 2 Section proceeded to the neighbourhood of BESACE FARM. In the early morning No. 1 Section advanced by OLGA HOUSES until CONDE HOUSE to positions about 200 yds behind the line. Two guns of No. 3 Section under 2/Lt. Hopwood proceeded on order from Bryan to DROP HOUSES for anti-aircraft work under Rt. 4. At 5.0pm remainder of No. 3 Section under 2/Lt. O.H. Davies advanced to LOUIS FARM and thence to neighbourhood. It was through REQUETE FARM, BESACE FARM and BOWER HOUSE. No 4 Section left MARSDIN FARM at 5.15pm to proceed to LOUIS FARM. As they were passing an 18 pounder limber near A Truck, a German shell struck the limber and all except 5 of the section and 2/Lt. Sly were wounded, badly wounded. One gun was destroyed while the other three were thrown into shell holes but afterwards recovered. This necessitated a fresh arrangement of the guns. Two guns of No. 1 Section under 2/Lt. Litken was ordered to advance behind the Reserve Companies of this battalion together with two guns of No. 2 Section under Sgt. Rumsent, while the remaining guns, two of No. 3 Section and two of No. 2 Section and two of No. 1 Section	

WAR DIARY
or
INTELLIGENCE SUMMARY.

Army Form C. 2118.

Place	Date	Hour	Summary of Events and Information	Remarks and references to Appendices
PILKEM-RIDGE	Oct.25th		were to move into and hold at all costs our original front line in case the attack proved a failure.	
"	" 26		Zero hour 5.40am. The infantry advanced about 600 yards then as all their Officers were killed or wounded, they began to retire and passed through the line of REQUETE FARM, BESACE FARM, BOWER HOUSE, S. of GRAVEL FARM, which had been consolidated under 2/Lt. O.K. Davies assisted by the guns under 2/Lt. Kitson and Sgt. Roberts. By noon only four guns remained, situated at the above mentioned farms.	
"	" 27		Company relieved by 171 M.G. Coy. Relief complete by 8.30 a.m. Company collected at HUDDLESTONE CORNER and proceeded to BOESINGHE, which they went by train to PROVEN to PILCH CAMP. The transport followed by road.	
PROVEN	" 28		General cleaning and examination of Gun equipment etc.	
"	" 29		Cleaning out inspection of Gun equipment etc.	
"	" 30		In reserve at PILCH CAMP, PROVEN.	
"	" 31		In reserve at PILCH CAMP, PROVEN. 61 Reinforcements reported from Base. Also 15 OR up after being back from Corps Reinforcement Camp.	

John M Cunningham
O.C. 170 M.G. Coy.

To Headquarters.
57th Division

1/12/17

War Diary

Herewith War Diary for month of November, 1917 for this Unit please.

[signature] Capt.
O.C. 170 M.G. COY.

WAR DIARY of the 170th MACHINE GUN COMPANY Army Form C. 2118.
INTELLIGENCE SUMMARY. IN THE FIELD. Nov. 1917.

(Erase heading not required.)

Vol 10

Place	Date	Hour	Summary of Events and Information	Remarks and references to Appendices
PROVEN	1.11.17		In Camp at Proven.	
"	2nd		do do do do	
"	3rd		do do do do . 2/Lt. G.A. Woodward and 2 teams of No 3 Section at LANGEMARCK on Anti-aircraft duty relieved by 2/Lt H. Dixon and 2 teams of No 4 Section.	
"	4th		In Camp at Proven.	
"	5th		do do do do	
"	6th		do do do do	
"	7th		do do do do	
LICQUES	8th		Company moved to LICQUES. (13 CHARS. NOORD. 3 F.25.44) Company by train to AUDRUIQ, thence by road together with Water Cart, Mess Cart and Mule Limbers. Remainder of transport by road.	
"	9th		In billets at LICQUES.	
"	10th		do do do do	
"	11th		do do do do	
"	12th		Company training.	
"	13th		do do	
"	14th		do do	
ECOTTES	15th		Company moved to ECOTTES. 3.F.17.22.(13 Calais 1/10000)	
"	16th		Company training.	
"	17th		do do do	
"	18th		do do do	

Army Form C. 2118.

WAR DIARY
or
INTELLIGENCE SUMMARY.
(Erase heading not required.)

Place	Date	Hour	Summary of Events and Information	Remarks and references to Appendices
ECOTTES	19th		Company Training. 32 men reported from Infantry Battalions for purpose of carriels.	
"	20th		Company Training. No 4 Section with 1/5th Loyal North Lancs Regt for attack practice.	
"	21st		do	
"	22nd		do . No 3 Section with 2/5 Loyal North Lancs Regt for attack practice	
"	23rd		do. No 1 Section with 2/6. Royal Innis. 6. I. Regt. for attack practice	
"	24th		do	
"	25th		do	
"	26th		do	
"	27th		do	
"	28th		Inspection by G.O.C. 57th Division	
"	29th		Company Training	
"	30		do	

O.C. 170 M.G. Coy.

To Headquarters
 57th Division

3.1.18

Herewith War Diary
for month of December
1917.

M Barum Lieut
O.C. 170 M.G. Coy.

WAR DIARY of 170 MACHINE GUN COMPANY.   Army Form C. 2118.

or

INTELLIGENCE SUMMARY.   IN THE FIELD.

(Erase heading not required.)

Place	Date	Hour	Summary of Events and Information	Remarks and references to Appendices
ECOTTES	Dec. 1		Company training.	
"	" 2		do do	
"	" 3		do do	
"	" 4		do do	
"	" 5		do do	
"	" 6		do do	
"	" 7		do do	
"	" 8		Transport left LOSTEBARN for trek to PROVEN area	
PROVEN	" 9		Company moved by motor buses to PLAISTOW CAMP, PROVEN. (Approx ref. 2.I.P.7.5.) where the Transport rejoined the Company	
"	" 10		Checking of Company material etc.	
"	" 11		Company training	
"	" 12		Company training. Transport moved to camp at I.H.15.00 (approx ref. ROUSBRUGGE)	
ROUSBRUGGE	" 13		Company moved to Camp at I.H.15.00 ROUSBRUGGE	
"	" 14		Company training	
"	" 15		do do	
BOESINGHE AREA	" 16		Transport and Adv. 1 and 2 sections moved by road to Box Camp A.11.6.10.50. (Ref.map. Belgium 25 N.W. 1/40000), BOESINGHE area. The 3 m.d.t sections proceeded	
"	" "		by rail from PROVEN to BOESINGHE station and then into line -	
"	" "		4 guns at PASCAL FARM (Ref.map m.p.Alguns U.12.C.50.20	
"	" "		2 guns at VEE BEND U.11.6.60.20	
"	" "		2 guns (A.A) at CANON FARM Belgium 25 N.W./40000 C.1.a.60.50.	

WAR DIARY

INTELLIGENCE SUMMARY

(Erase heading not required.)

Army Form C. 2118.

Place	Date	Hour	Summary of Events and Information	Remarks and references to Appendices
BUSINGHE AREA	Dec 17		Company training with Nos 1 and 2 Sections and three men of Nos 3 and 4 Sections. Situation normal. Harassing fire carried out by guns at PASCAL FARM both night and day.	
"	18		Situation normal. Harassing fire as before.	
"	19		Inspection relief. Harassing fire on NIEUWEMOLEN at NIEUWEMOLEN my ref. 0.36.c.10.50 and 0.36.c.50.30.)	
"	20		Situation normal	
"	21		Situation normal	
"	22		Raid by Germans on TURENNE CROSSING VI.d.10.25. 5000 rounds fired by S.O.S. guns at PASCAL FARM and VEE BEND.	
"	23		Situation normal. Harassing fire.	
"	24		Guns at PASCAL FARM and VEE BEND relieved by 172 M.G.Cy. Guns at CANON FARM relieved by 2 Lewis Guns of 171 Bn.	
"	25		Xmas parades	
"	26		Company training class of 1 June etc	
"	27		Company training	
"	28		do	
"	29		do	
"	30		Packing of limbers etc preparatory to move on Dec 31st	
"	31		Company and Transport moved to Hills at PORTLAND CAMP. Bivouac along (Map ref. N37c40.60 Sheet 19).	

[signature]

Army Form C. 2118.

WAR DIARY
or
INTELLIGENCE SUMMARY.
(Erase heading not required.)

170 M.G. Coy

1/1/12

Place	Date	Hour	Summary of Events and Information	Remarks and references to Appendices
PROVEN AREA	Jan 1		Coy in Pollard Camp. Transport lies 2 limbers, water cart, mess cart and 5 officers which by land to GODE AREA	
	2		Coy moved to ERQUINGHEM by rail - entrainment leaving Proving at 6.40 a.m. (A.M.P. HAZEBROUCK) 8.40 a.m. detrained at PROVEN at 9 am - arrived at BAILLEUL WEST at 12.30 p.m. making rail & tramway to Laundry. Equipment 36 NW H 57 5.7 (100000)	
			Transport moved from GODE area to 0.28 b to 00 (36 NW) than to LA HAYE FARM by rail, the transport entrained at PROVEN 10 a.m. detrained at BAILLEUL WEST and proceeded by road to camp, ERQUINGHEM.	
ERQUINGHEM	3		No. 1, 2 & 3 sections relieved three sections of 10th Australian M.G. Coy in the CHAPELLE D'ARMENTIÈRES sector of the BOIS GRENIER line. Tripods and belts were taken over. Relief complete by 8 pm	
			Disposition of Company - Headquarters and section in centre at H 5 d. 10. 50 (36 NW) No 1 section in right subsector, section Headquarters in Subsidiary line at B 30 c 5.8. 2 guns in subway, 1 gun in support line, No 2 section in Centre subsector, section	

WAR DIARY
or
INTELLIGENCE SUMMARY

Army Form C. 2118.

Place	Date	Hour	Summary of Events and Information	Remarks and references to Appendices
BRAQUINAGHIEN	Oct 3		Arrived Station in at Trd Q.8.2 commenced unloading our stuff	
			The estimate of shelter existing doesn't at Trd Q.8 in civilian use. 2 men billeting parts and 3 in report line	
			Remainder at H.Q. 2.30	
WELNAMAN SECTOR	4		Situation normal	
	5		Situation normal. In accordance with instructions issued from	
			9 @ Royal Fd. 2 guns were withdrawn from support line and placed in	
			RUE FLEURIE Sector with H.Q. at LA VESEE E.17.c.10.75	
			4 section guns 2 RUE FLEURIE ?.17.a.? 2 guns subsidiary line	
			2 section guns on subsidiary line. Our support line	
			3 section guns in subsidiary line and 2 guns in support line	
	6		Situation normal. 750 rounds ?.?.? fired ?.?.? Enemy Saprs Posn. SUPPORT FARM	
			Situation normal. 750 rounds fired from O.P. of I.9.c.45.15 on WEZ ENEMY FRONT & REST ROADS.	
	7		1000 rounds fired from O.P. I.9.c.45.15 I.8.6095	
	8		Situation normal. 1750 rounds fired from I.9.c.45.15 on Tr.d. 31	
			?NEZMAQUHART ?.?.? I.3.75	

WAR DIARY or INTELLIGENCE SUMMARY

Army Form C. 2118.

Place	Date	Hour	Summary of Events and Information	Remarks and references to Appendices
MARTINPUICH SECTOR	10		Situation normal. No S.O.S. station allowed to be at station.	
			Situation normal. 1500 rounds fired from L14d 57.31 on Incubator Trench I33d 30.80.	
	11		Situation normal. 750 rounds fired from I14d 57.31 on Trench I33b 0.10 – I33d 30.80.	
			Situation normal. 1000 rounds fired from E29 45.15 on "WEZ MACQUART X ROADS".	
	12		Situation normal. 1000 rounds fired from E29 45.15 on WEZ MACQUART X ROADS. 750 rounds fired from I14d 57.31 on Incomplete trench L33d 35.15 – I33d 50.75.	
	13		Situation normal. 1000 rounds fired from E29 45.15 on WEZ MACQUART X ROADS. 1000 rounds fired from I14d 57.31 on Incomplete trench I33d 3585 – I33d 53.75.	
	14		Situation normal. 750 rounds fired from E29 45.15 on WEZ MACQUART X ROADS. 750 rounds fired from I14d 57.31 on Incubator Trench I33b 30.10 – I33d 30.50.	
	15		Situation normal. 750 rounds on Incubator Trench I33b 30.16 – I33d 30.80.	
	16		Situation normal. No S.O.S station as yet. No S.O.S station.	
	17		1000 rounds fired on LARGES FM DISTILLERY	
	18		Situation normal.	
			Situation normal. 9000 rounds from E29 45.87 on Dump E22d 65.35. 1000 rounds from I29 45.15 on Dump I22b 65.35. 3000 rounds from I29 11.11 in Dump I22 b 65.35. 1000 rounds from I30 d 15.36 on F27d 70.30. 1000 rounds fm	
			I14 d45 42 in trench. I23 – 0-0 20. 1000 rounds from I14 d 45 42	

WAR DIARY or INTELLIGENCE SUMMARY

Army Form C. 2118.

(Erase heading not required.)

Place	Date	Hour	Summary of Events and Information	Remarks and references to Appendices
WEZ MACQUART SECTOR	June 18	10.25	On I.7.b.10.25.	
	19		Situation normal. 1000 rounds fired in I.2.b.4.7.4.1.	
	20		Situation normal.	
	21		Situation normal. 750 a.m. rounds at Snipers. 1000 rounds on INCOMPLETE DRIVE.	
			E.23.b.4.7.7.1.	
	22		Situation normal. 150 rounds fired 50 x from I.P. & I.10.2.	
	23		Situation normal. 1 & 1 Rattan Wood.	
			1000 rounds fired on PARADISE ROAD. 1050 rounds fired on SNIPERS HOUSE.	
			1500 rounds at enemy planes.	
	24		Situation normal. 500 rounds fired at gust-army planes.	
	25		Situation normal.	
	26		Situation normal.	
	27		Situation normal.	
	28		Situation normal. 3000 rounds at enemy planes.	
	29		Situation normal. 500 rounds at enemy planes. 1000 rounds on	
	30		WEZ MACQUART. 1000 rounds on PARADISE DISTILLERY X ROADS.	
			Situation normal. 19 H Section relieved by D.I. Section.	
			3000 rounds in connection with recoopation of left Brigade.	
	31		Situation normal.	

O.B.Brown 2/Lt
acting O.C. 170 M.G. COY.

WAR DIARY
INTELLIGENCE SUMMARY

Army Form C. 2118.

A Coy 57th Batt. N.S.W.

Place	Date	Hour	Summary of Events and Information	Remarks and references to Appendices
WEZ MACKWT SECTOR	FEB 1		Situation normal. 23750 rounds fired in Garrison m.g. nest	
"	2		Situation normal. 500 rounds fired on Distilling Road	
	3		Situation normal. 1000 rounds fired on incident Alley, 1000 rounds on Distilling Road, 1000 rounds Iverson Avenue, 1000 rounds on Wez Macquart X Roads	
	4		Situation normal. 2000 rounds fired on Large Farm & Brewery, 6000 rounds on Distilling Road, 1000 rounds on Large Farm	
	5		Situation normal. 1000 rounds fired on Large Farm & 1000 rounds at Irving Plus 9. No 4 sector relieved No 3 Section on Coy sector. No 3 Return to the Landries H.S. a. 5.7 when they on held in reserve under D.M.G.O.	
	6		Situation normal. 1000 rounds fired on Large Farm	
	7		Situation normal. 1000 rounds fired on Paradise Road and fired at I.w.2 d.o 35 to I.28.d 70.98, 750 hours on Deadleg Road, 2 1000 rounds on Vicar Roads at 9.33 a 60.80	
	8		Situation normal. 1000 rounds fired on Paradise Rd Bend I.13.d 70.90. 1000 rounds on Large Farm	
	9		Situation normal. 2000 rounds fired on Paradise Rd & Trench 1000 rounds on Trench I.22.a.15.14, 1000 rounds T.21.d 01.28	

WAR DIARY
or
INTELLIGENCE SUMMARY.
(Erase heading not required.)

Army Form C. 2118.

Place	Date	Hour	Summary of Events and Information	Remarks and references to Appendices
WEZ MACQUART SECTOR	Feb 10		Situation Normal. 1500 rounds fired on T.16.d.02.10, 1500 rounds on T.16.d.30.60, 2500 rounds on T.27.b.27.20 - 1000 rounds T.21.d.61.23, 1000 rounds on T.21.C.14.78. Harassing fire in connection with forthcoming raid.	
	11		Situation Normal. 3500 rounds fired on T.22.C.85.75, 3500 rounds on T.16.d.02.10, 3000 rounds on T.16.d.30.60, 3000 rounds T.21.b.47.20 - Minor operation carried out without success.	
	12		Situation Normal. 1000 rounds fired on Parada Road. 170. M.G. Company were relieved by 115. M.G. Coy in the WEZ MACQUART Sub-Sec. Relief complete. Company marched by sections to Estaires. Transport less fighting limbers by road to Estaires. Location of the Company HQ & No 1 & No 2 Sections L.29 & 95.00, No 3 & No 4 Sections L.29 & 90.40. Orderly Room L.29.d.70.40 Transport L.28.d.50.40	
	13		Company in billets. Cleaning up.	
	14		Company in billets.	
	15		Company training. Telegraph Recon positions. No 1 Section Bridgehurts R.17.a.4.9 - R.11.d.1.8 - R.11.C.0.5 R.10.a.4.7, No 2 Section Clifton group No 3 Section Ruy Barllent group No 4 Section fro reserve at L.35.C.3.1 Advanced by HQ L.34 & 70.60	

WAR DIARY
or
INTELLIGENCE SUMMARY

Army Form C. 2118.

Place	Date	Hour	Summary of Events and Information	Remarks and references to Appendices
WEZ MACQUARIE SECTOR	16		Company Training	
	17		Company in Billets. General cleaning of Equipment etc. Football	
	18		Company Training. Two A.A. guns mounted at 2.29 d 3.5 and 2.29 d 6.6. (36 A.N.E. 1/40000)	
	19		Company Training. Opposition added to 9 wood. Two Approves A.	
	20		Company Training	
	21		Company Training	
	22		Company Training	
	23		Company Training. A.A. gun positions bombed over Co Lewis Guns 172 2/1 Bn.	
	24		Company Training	
	25		Company Training. No 1 Section Application & Group firing practices on 25" Rifle Range	
	26		Company Training. No 3 Section on Rifle Range	
	27		Company Training. No 4 Section on Rifle Range	
	28		Company Training. No 2 Section on Rifle Range	

T/8 Stevens Bt
Capt.
O.C. 170 M.G. COY.

WAR DIARY APPENDIX A
INTELLIGENCE SUMMARY
(Erase heading not required.)

Army Form C. 2118.

Place	Date	Hour	Summary of Events and Information	Remarks and references to Appendices
ESTAIRES			Reference Maps 36.N.W. 36 S.W. 36A N.E. 36A S.E. Operation Order No 9. (1) In the event of the enemy breaking through the Portuguese front the 170th Machine Gun Company will recept and be responsible for the defence of the following points:- Right Sub-sector CLIFTON SOUTH 1 gun, CLIFTON CENTRE 1 gun, CLIFTON NORTH 1 gun, RIEZ BAILLEUL GROUP 4 guns. BRIDGEHEADS:- R.17.a.4.7. 2 guns. R.11.c.1.8. 1 gun. R.11.c.0.8. 1 gun. R.10.a.4.7. 1 gun. 4 guns in reserve at L.35.c.3.1. (2) Advanced Company Headquarters will be at R.12.a.5.5. with the Right Battalion Headquarters. (3) On receipt of order "D.S. ACTION" sections will proceed immediately to position detailed as under:- No 1 Section R.10.a.4.7. 1 gun. R.17.a.4.9. 2 guns No 2 Section R.11.d.1.8. 1 gun CLIFTON SOUTH 1 gun CLIFTON CENTRE 1 gun. CLIFTON NORTH 1 gun No 3 Section RIEZ BAILLEUL GROUP 4 guns No 4 Section in reserve at L.35.c.3.1. 4 guns. (4) S.A.A. At each of these positions there is a reserve of 5000 rounds of S.A.A. (5) Filling limbers will always be packed ready for this move. It is necessary for purposes of training to keep Subs. Tripods and Spare parts box at Company Headquarters. On receipt of an "D.S. ACTION" Transport Officer will immediately and all fighting limbers to their company Headquarters. Section Officers will then take control	

APPENDIX A (Page II)

(5) of their timbers, road from Bispots. Opens fronts have as quickly as possible and proceed independently by sections to position detailed.

(6) As soon as sections are in position, section Officers will report by runner to advanced Company Head quarters, near the Cross Road "HOME".

(7) Section Officers are reminded that as soon as they leave Estaires they are liable to be engaged in open warfare, and will handle their sections to the best tactical advantage. They must however, make every effort to occupy the positions detailed.

(8) All sections must be ready to move within 15 minutes of receipt of order "D.S. ACTION".

(9) DRESS: Battle Order; packs carried in the limbers.

(10) The Infantry on the right Sub Sector will be 1/4th Batt: South Lancs Regt.

(11) 172 M.G. Company will be responsible for Machine Gun defence of the Left Sub Sector.

B.E.F. FRANCE & FLANDERS
THIRD ARMY. TROOPS.

CASUALTY CLEARING
STATIONS.
NO 3 CASUALTY CLEARING

1914 OCT TO 1919 MAY.

B.E.F. FRANCE & FLANDERS.
THIRD ARMY. TROOPS.

CASUALTY CLEARING
STATIONS.
NO 3 CASUALTY CLEARING
1914 OCT TO 1919 MAY.

www.ingramcontent.com/pod-product-compliance
Lightning Source LLC
Chambersburg PA
CBHW081442160426
43193CB00013B/2355